The Gate
Vegetarian
Cookbook

The Gate

Vegetarian Cookbook

Where Asia meets the Mediterranean

Adrian and Michael Daniel

With Lewis Esson   Photographs by Georgia Glynn Smith   MITCHELL BEAZLEY

The Gate Vegetarian Cookbook
by Adrian and Michael Daniel with Lewis Esson

First published in Great Britain in 2004
by Mitchell Beazley, an imprint of Octopus Publishing
Group Ltd, 2-4 Heron Quays,
London E14 4JP

A CIP catalogue record for this book is available
from the British Library.

ISBN 1 84000 837 7

Commissioning Editor: Rebecca Spry
Executive Art Editor: Yasia Williams
Photographs: Georgia Glynn Smith
Food preparation: Adrian Daniel
Design: Grade Design Consultants, London
Editor: Susan Fleming
Proofreader: Julie Tolley
Index: John Noble
Production: Sarah Rogers

Typeset in Vag Rounded and Dinn

Printed and bound by Toppan Printing Company
in China

Contents

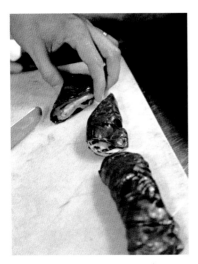

Introduction

We were lucky enough to grow up in a family environment in which good food was important. Our grandmother, who presided over the preparation of family meals in our home, was an awe-inspiring cook. Epitomizing the richly varied Indo-Iraqi tradition of our heritage, everything she cooked seemed of another time, another place. She would often start preparing food days ahead of the meal for which it was intended, working from early in the morning to late in the day, cooking everything with infinite care.

Our grandmother seemed to love feeding other people, but ate little herself. She was happy to stand at the kitchen doorway watching others enjoy her creations. We like to think that some of our success as restaurateurs comes from her spirit.

When we turned vegetarian as teenagers, it was quite a challenge, as vegetarianism was so alien to our culture. Adrian, in particular, really didn't care much for vegetables – a dislike that sprang from the "wetness" of the usual boiled veg. So, mostly in the spirit of self-preservation, he set about creating his own ways of cooking with vegetables, usually involving roasting, frying or grilling. From this early experimentation – marrying his ideas with the spicing of our grandmother's traditional Indo-Iraqi dishes and with his own experiences of food in the Mediterranean, California and other parts of the world – he developed his own very particular cuisine, which is still evolving.

One of our first ventures in catering was at the Glastonbury Festival. We arrived with two big pots of soup, a spirit burner, some jerry cans

and little else. After being ignored for most of the first day, Michael started shouting "Get your spinach dhal here... " and, lo and behold, business began to pick up. The next day people were coming back asking if we had any more. It was our first lesson in marketing.

A few years later, while looking for a job in food, Adrian came across the Christian Community in Hammersmith, who were looking for someone to run their cafeteria. We subsequently took it over and the Gate Restaurant was born. No-one was more surprised than us when it became so successful, and only three years later we received the *Time Out* Eating and Drinking Award for the Best Vegetarian Meal, which was more than we could ever have hoped for. We thought ourselves – and still do – incredibly lucky that we could carry on doing something that gave us such satisfaction.

We like to share our enthusiasms and discoveries with our customers. We love fungi foraging, and so started our annual fungi fest in 1997. When we travel abroad on holiday we look for new ingredients and dishes to bring back to the restaurant for our regulars. Many of them are also constant sources of inspiration, and fascinating founts of the most arcane wisdom. We hope that some of all this will come across to those who read this book and we offer you our recipes and what goes with them in the spirit of our grandmother, standing at the doorway watching others enjoy.

Adrian and Michael Daniel,
London, 2004

Gate Store Cupboard

We don't for one minute want you to think that in order to cook our sort of food you need to have everything mentioned here to hand. Instead, this is intended merely as a sort of *aide-memoire* and guide to the ingredients that we tend to use all the time.

Aromatics

The first things to run through are, in fact, not strictly speaking store cupboard ingredients. These are the (mostly fresh) aromatics that we use as the bases for most savoury dishes. Apart from the obvious *onions* and *garlic*, we often use *red onions*, particularly when we want sweetness, and *shallots* for their intensity of flavour and extra hint of garlic. We generally favour the large banana shallots for their mild sweetness and because they are less laborious to peel as you need fewer of them. Another member of the onion family that we use a lot as a basic flavouring is the *leek*, for its mild subtle flavour. We also tend to add *celery* to our basic aromatic mixtures for its simple intense "greenness". When you are preparing such veg, don't throw away the trimmings, but use them to make stock (see page 40).

We use a wide variety of *chillies*, from the common little red bird's-eye chillies, which have a good mix of chilli taste and moderate peppery heat, to chipotles, the Mexican smoked jalapeños, for their rich complex flavours. Apart from in some traditional Indo-Iraqi dishes, we generally remove the pale membranes and seeds inside chillies that hold most of the capsaicin, the heat-producing oil, as we don't want the flavours of our dishes to be drowned out by the heat. When you are seeding chillies, wear rubber gloves or be sure to wash your hands immediately afterwards, as the capsaicin can linger and burn your skin if you touch a sensitive part.

One of the things that really differentiates a lot of our savoury dishes is our frequent addition of *fresh root ginger* and *galangal*, its milder cousin, which are usually limited to Oriental cooking. Both keep well in the freezer and can be grated straight from frozen.

Finally, those most common of all flavourings: *salt* and *pepper*. Like most cooks nowadays, we use sea salt and freshly ground black pepper (or white pepper where you don't want a pale dish to look speckly), and it is amazing what a difference this can make to the clarity of the finished taste of a dish. Ready-ground pepper really has very little flavour, as it has lost most of its essential oils by the time it gets on the shelf. Try to get those little hessian bags of black peppercorns from India, as these really have a wonderful flavour.

Herbs

We use a wide range of fresh herbs. *Bay leaves*, *parsley* (usually flat-leaved), *thyme* and *rosemary* in particular give depth of flavour to many of our recipes. The more distinctive tangs of *mint*, *basil* and *oregano* are also among our favourites in appropriate dishes. *Chives* we tend to add at the last minute so as not to cook out their delicate onion flavour, or we use the stalks, whole or snipped, for garnish. Fresh *coriander leaves* are probably our favourite herb but, as with chives, we usually add them late in the cooking to keep their full flavour. If we want to incorporate the flavour earlier on in the cooking, we use the roots and stalks. (If you buy your herbs from a good greengrocer or street market, rather than a

supermarket, you'll usually get bunches of coriander complete with roots.)

For dishes that are more Oriental in style, we use Thai or holy *basil*, which has a characteristic clovey warmth, *curry leaves* for their subtle pungency, *lemongrass* for its delicious perfumed sourness and *lime leaves* for their intense floral-citrus hit.

Much as we prefer to use fresh herbs wherever possible, we do use some *dried herbs*, such as dried bay leaves, lime leaves, oregano, rosemary and thyme, as these keep a good strong flavour when dried – and some even develop an extra quality that further develops in long slow cooking.

As with aromatic vegetables, when you are preparing fresh herbs, don't discard any of the trimmed-off stems, stalks and roots, but instead add these to the stockpot (see page 40).

Spices

Our spicing is probably what we are best known for, although we always assert that the distinctive and unusual tastes of our food are down to a combination of spices and fresh flavours – i.e. our aromatics and herbs – and not just due to spices alone.

Some spices we use fairly regularly, including the classic range of hot and warming ones, such as *dried chillies, cinnamon, cloves, nutmeg* and *ground ginger*. Others we value for their subtlety (and the colour they impart), such as *saffron* and *turmeric*, and yet others for their very distinctive taste notes, such as *coriander seeds* for their unique lemony/sagey flavour, *cumin* for its peppery nuttiness, *fenugreek* for its bitter-sweetness, *smoked paprika* for that very smokiness, and *star anise* for its liquorice overtones.

There are several spices and spice mixtures that we normally employ only when they are appropriate to a particular cuisine, such as *Cajun spice mix* – a heady blend of onion, garlic, chillies, mustard seeds, paprika, cumin and peppercorns with various dried herbs. Perhaps most important are those spices most closely associated with Indian cooking, such as *onion seeds* and *white and black sesame seeds*, as well as Indian spice mixes such as *panch phoran* – cumin, fennel seeds, mustard

seeds, nigella and fenugreek – and, of course, the invaluable *garam masala*, that rich blend of cinnamon, bay, cumin, coriander seeds, black and white cardamom seeds, peppercorns, cloves and mace.

Apart from ground ginger (which we only use to reinforce the flavour of fresh root or stem ginger), we have little time for ready-ground spices as they have usually lost most of their essential oils by the time they get to you. Instead we always first roast the whole seeds, flakes, sticks, etc. in a dry pan until they give off their aromas to develop their full flavour and then we either pound them using a pestle and mortar or grind them ourselves in an electric coffee-grinder.

If you are buying a spice mix, again try to get mixes that consist of the whole seeds, etc., or, in the case of items such as garam masala, say, a paste of the spices pulverized in oil retains a good true strong flavour.

Flavourings

Of course, there are all those other assorted store cupboard ingredients you need that add to the taste in cooking but aren't herbs or spices. They are a bit of a ragbag, but probably principal among them for us are *dried mushrooms*, notably ceps. Dried wild mushrooms of all sorts can be extremely useful for those months when you can't get them fresh. They may not have the texture of the original when rehydrated, but they still pack a powerful flavour, and the soaking water makes a useful stock.

Also fairly indispensable are some *olives*, usually stoned black, and those pungent little flavour-bombs, *capers*. Buy the latter packed in salt for an infinitely superior flavour to the brine-packed ones. *Tamarind* concentrate is also a useful flavouring to have, the intense sweet-sour fruity flavour being useful for curries and lots of Eastern dishes.

Condiments such as *mustard* – we find French Dijon most useful – also often serve as flavourings. As does *horseradish*, both preserved in vinegar and dried for when you can't get the fresh root, as well as *wasabi*, the Japanese equivalent, which comes in handy little sachets. On the subject of Japanese food, we also keep *miso*, the fermented soy bean paste at the heart of many an Oriental soup or sauce – both as tubs of the paste and as sachets of dried powder – and packs of ready-toasted sheets of *nori*, the dried seaweed used to wrap sushi, as well as jars of the *pickled pink ginger* served with it.

Our Middle Eastern roots and our love of flowery perfumed flavours mean that we always have to hand bottles of *orange blossom water* and *rose water*, which are as useful in rich complex savoury dishes as they are in sweet. For sweet dishes, we also try to keep *lavender flowers*, dried or fresh when available. Other invaluable flavourings for desserts include bottles of stem ginger in syrup, whole *vanilla pods* – try to get the intensely flavoured thin Bourbon ones from Madagascar – and, of course, good-quality *dark chocolate* with at least 70 per cent cocoa solids.

Oils and vinegars

These are the most basic components of flavour, and items that it is simply foolish to stint on, as a poor-quality oil will mar the taste of any dish, no matter how good the other ingredients. We generally cook in either *vegetable oil* or *olive oil*, depending on the dish, reserving extra-virgin olive oil for dishes to which the oil is added later, such as a dressing, or in which the oil used for cooking will actually form a significant part of the finished sauce.

We use *groundnut oil* for most stir-frying and for deep-frying, as it has a good neutral flavour and can take the high temperatures involved. We do occasionally also use *sesame oil* for stir-frying and other forms of Oriental dishes, although toasted sesame oil is more generally added at the last minute as a dressing – but be careful, as its strong flavour can easily drown the other flavours. Some oils are used – again judiciously – almost entirely for their flavour, notably mustard oil, walnut oil and, of course, truffle oil.

For salad dressings, etc., we use either *white wine vinegar* or *balsamic vinegar*, depending on the other ingredients. The cheaper balsamic vinegars are a waste of money as they are mostly caramel; spend that little bit extra for the real thing and you have an

instant delectable sauce in your cupboard. *Rice vinegar* is used in many Oriental dishes, so it is also a good idea to have some of that.

Cans, tubes, jars, etc

Now for the real "store cupboard" items, the things that are so convenient for putting together quick meals. Always have several cans of *chopped tomatoes*, which are handy for all sorts of things, from stews to pasta sauces. Go for Italian brands that use plum tomatoes, as these often have a better flavour than many of the fresh tomatoes you can buy in this country. *Canned pulses* are also always useful, especially butter beans, cannellini beans, red kidney beans and chickpeas. *Coconut milk* is useful for Thai and other Asian dishes – if you let the can settle for a week or two, the thick top layer that forms inside can be used as coconut cream.

In jars we would always have *sun-dried tomatoes in oil* and *tahini*, the thick *sesame seed paste*. We couldn't be without tubes of tomato purée (keep them in the fridge once open); the little cans are fiddly and the purée doesn't keep so well in them once opened. Bottles of *Tabasco*, *Worcestershire* and *soy sauce* (Kikkoman is our favourite) are essential flavourings and condiments, and some *Thai fish sauce* will come in handy for many Asian dishes.

Perhaps most important of all are some good-quality vegetable stock cubes and/or a drum of the invaluable *Marigold vegetable bouillon powder*. Recently Knorr have started doing an excellent cep stock cube, but these are still fairly difficult to find in the UK.

Rice, grains and pulses

If you are going to cook an international array of dishes, you need to equip yourself with all the types of *rice*: a good-quality basmati for Indian-type dishes, Japanese rice for sushi, Thai fragrant rice for South-East Asian and other Oriental dishes and, of course, a risotto rice, such as *arborio*, *vialone nano* or *carnaroli*.

You'll need a good strong bread flour if you are going to make bread, *Italian "00" (doppio zero) flour* for pasta, some *chapati flour* and a pack of cornflour for thickening sauces and stews. Of course, for bread you'll also need active dry yeast. A packet of *dried breadcrumbs* is also handy for coating food to be fried. Packs of pre-cooked *couscous* and *polenta* allow you to give interest to side dishes, and are quick and easy to prepare.

No store cupboard would be complete without a selection of *noodles* and other *pasta*. Flat noodles such as tagliatelle, as well as being a basis for a pasta meal, work well as an accompaniment to any dish in a creamy sauce. Also having some Oriental noodles, both egg and the flat rice type (rice sticks) puts you in a good position to conjure up a fast meal.

Dried pulses are always handy: we always have chickpeas, packs of green, red and tasty little Puy lentils and yellow split peas. Try to buy these from a Middle Eastern or Asian shop as otherwise they may have been mouldering on the shelf for some time, losing much of their flavour and goodness, and they will take far too long to cook.

Dried fruits and nuts

We make a lot of use of dried fruits in sweet and savoury dishes as they are so convenient and intense in flavour. We always have to hand *dried dates, apricots, figs* and *apples* as well, of course, as *sultanas* and *prunes*, usually the delicious Agen prunes from France. When buying dried fruit it is best to go for organic, or at least get it from a health-food store, as many everyday brands are coated in preservatives and oil, the taste of which can really mar a dish.

Nuts are also staples for us and we use *almonds, hazelnuts, macadamia nuts, peanuts, pecans, pine nuts, pistachios* and *walnuts* regularly. Try to buy your nuts as whole as possible; we know it is a fiddle to shell and skin them, but the flavour is so much better.

Sweeteners

Whenever possible, sweeteners should add flavour as well as sweetness. Demerara sugar is our number one choice and we use the unrefined muscovado and palm sugar (jaggery) for strongly-flavoured and Asian dishes. Icing sugar is also essential for flavouring fruit purées

and dusting over desserts and baked goods. Good floral runny honey (with not too distinctive a flavour) is also vital, and maple syrup is good to have for its particularly voluptuous richness.

Liquors

Whether or not you drink them, some alcoholic beverages are essential in the kitchen (and, if it is of concern to you, the alcohol itself is usually driven off in the cooking). We recommend you have *Armagnac*, *Madeira* and *Marsala*, which all give good depth of flavour to appropriate sweet and savoury dishes. *Grand Marnier* often also comes in handy for flavouring desserts. You don't have to buy whole bottles; half or quarter bottles or miniatures will do. Of course, you will almost certainly need a good *dry white wine* and, occasionally, a *fruity red wine*, but we don't think of these as store cupboard items – and don't treat them as such; an opened bottle of wine that has sat around for too long will be vinegary and harsh, and will certainly not enhance food to which it is added. Do keep a couple of cans or bottles of beer for making batters – *Japanese beer* if you're making tempura, and don't forget some *mirin*, Japanese sweet rice wine, for sushi and lots of other uses.

Soups

With regard to soup, our philosophy goes back to something Mahatma Gandhi famously said: "Drink your food and eat your soup." In other words, make sure your food is properly chewed for the sake of the digestion, and your soups are chunky enough to be filling. At home, soups were always made in extra-large quantities on Fridays for the whole weekend, so they were generally seen as a bit of a treat, an attitude we still hold on to.

Soups are constant very good sellers in both restaurants. We do try to keep all the soups vegan, but when making them at home we will use butter and possibly cream. The soups on the menu very much reflect the season and the weather - refreshingly pungent Thai soups or chilled well puréed beetroot cutta swathed in soured cream in summer, and the usual comforters in winter. One of our favourite regular customers, a venerable Egyptian Jew, likes to have soup as dessert, so he just loves our summer menus as he can have hot soup to begin with and a cold soup to finish.

Obviously most good soups need a good stock (page 40) and we keep all our vegetable and herb trimmings, such as celery tops and coriander roots, for stock, as they help boost its flavour. Don't spoil a soup by using it to mop up old and/or second-rate veg (although you could put such stuff in the stock pot), as the soup needs to sing of the vegetables' freshness. As you will see, we often use extra-strongly flavoured veg, such as celery and Jerusalem artichokes, as a base for soups containing other vegetables, to give a greater depth of flavour and texture.

Finally, remember that when you are blending soups, most ordinary domestic food processors just aren't up to the job, and give you results that either separate or are full of torn fibres. Instead, use a stick blender and remember to hold it at a slight angle to get a good flow of the soup into its blades.

Beetroot Cutta with Kubba

The term "cutta" comes from "cutter", meaning "sour" in Arabic. This traditional Indo-Iraqi soup is served with or without *kubba* (semolina dumplings). The *kubba* filling can be made a little ahead or frozen (freeze any left over for your next soup). If you have time, half-freezing the filling makes it easier to work with.

SERVES 6-8

55g (2oz) butter
1 large onion, finely chopped
1 tbsp finely chopped garlic
2 tbsp finely chopped fresh
　root ginger
handful each of mint and coriander
　leaves, plus extra for garnish
1kg (2¼lb) raw beetroot, sliced
6 celery stalks, roughly chopped
1 medium potato, diced

2 tbsp sugar
1.5 litres (2¾ pints) vegetable stock
　(page 40)
salt and black pepper

KUBBA
250g (9oz) semolina
125g (4½oz) rice flour
pinch each of salt, garam masala
　and chopped coriander

KUBBA FILLING
½ onion, puréed
2 tbsp olive oil
1 garlic clove, crushed
small knob of fresh root ginger, grated
½ carrot and 1 celery stalk, grated
small handful each of mint and
　coriander leaves, chopped
handful of soft breadcrumbs
juice of ½ lemon

1 | Melt the butter in a large pan and gently sauté the onion, garlic, ginger and mint until softened. Add the remaining ingredients with seasoning to taste and bring to the boil. Cover and simmer for 1 hour, or until the beetroot is completely soft.

2 | While the soup is simmering, prepare the *kubba*. In a bowl, mix all the ingredients together with just enough cold water to form a loose dough. Leave in a warm place for about 30 minutes to let the flours absorb the water.

3 | Meanwhile, make the *kubba* filling. Squeeze any excess juice from the onion purée. Heat the oil in a frying pan and cook the onion gently until softened. Add the garlic and ginger and cook for a minute, then stir in the carrot and celery and cook for 6-7 minutes until they are softened. Off the heat stir in the herbs, breadcrumbs and a good squeeze of lemon juice.

4 | When the filling is cool enough to handle, make the *kubba*. With wet hands, take a walnut-sized piece of the *kubba* mix and mould into a flat disc in the palm of the hand. Place a similarly sized piece of filling in the centre of the dough round and fold it up and around the stuffing, using a little more water to seal the edges if necessary. Twist off any excess dough at the top. Repeat until all the dough and filling are used – you need to make at least 12-14 *kubba* (freeze any filling left over).

5 | Drop the dumplings into the soup and simmer very gently for 10-15 minutes, stirring from time to time, until the dough is cooked.

6 | Put 2-3 *kubba* in the bottom of each bowl, adjust the seasoning of the soup if necessary, pour it over and garnish with the extra shredded herbs to serve.

1 | 2 |
3 | 4
| 5

Dumplings (Kubba)

Dumplings are a feature of most peasant cooking, being an excellent and inexpensive way of extending – and adding interest to – all sorts of dishes, particularly soups and stews. Usually called *"kofta"* in the Arab world and the Indian subcontinent, we called them *"kubba"* (from the Arabic for ball-shaped), while the Syrians know them as *"kibbeh"*, and the Egyptians as *"kobeba"*.

Claudia Roden in *The Book of Jewish Food* says, interestingly, that these dumplings were the means by which women were once judged as cooks (even if their servants cooked them), and in certain circles the dumplings became incredibly refined and elegant. Fillings were, of course, generally based on meat, especially lamb, but the flavourings could vary widely. In our house they were a weekend treat, reserved for Sunday best – sort of our version of Yorkshire pudding – and a soup was too wet without them.

In a bowl, mix all the outer shell ingredients together with just enough cold water to form a loose dough. Leave the dough in a warm place for approximately 30 minutes to let the flours absorb the water.

Meanwhile, make the filling and, when it is cool enough to handle, make the *kubba*.

1 | With wet hands, take a walnut-sized piece of the *kubba* mix and mould into a flat disc in the palm of the hand.

2 | Place a similarly sized piece of filling in the centre of the dough round.

3 | Fold the dough up and around the stuffing, using a little more water to seal the edges, if necessary; twist off any excess dough at the top.

4 | Roll the dough back into a sealed ball. Repeat until all the dough and filling are used (freeze any filling left over).

5 | Simmer the *kubba* in the soup gently for 10-15 minutes, stirring from time to time, until the dough is cooked.

Bamia Cutta

(Okra Soup)

Our family would eat *cutta* on most weekends. Okra was a traditional vegetable for the dish in our household. We're not sure where our parents found it when they first came to London – it is possible they found it, even then, in the Ridley Road market, but we think they probably used tinned.

SERVES 4

½ recipe quantity *kubba* prepared
  with filling (see page 20)
a little vegetable oil
200g (7oz) okra, trimmed of
  the stalk ends but kept intact
salt
1 large onion, finely chopped
2-3 fat garlic cloves, finely chopped

2.5cm (1in) chunk fresh root
  ginger, grated
3-4 celery stalks, cut lengthwise
  into strips, leaves reserved and
  chopped
1 red pepper, seeded, layer of flesh
  removed, then cut into strips
1 x 400g can chopped tomatoes

200ml (7fl oz) vegetable stock
  (page 40)
salt and black pepper

1 | Make the *kubba* (see page 20). Coat the bottom of a large frying pan with oil and get it good and hot. Add the okra with a touch of salt and toss over a high heat until slightly softened. This helps to reduce the "goopiness" when they are cut or bitten into.

2 | In another pan, soften the onion in a little oil, then add the garlic and ginger and sweat for a minute or two. Add the celery with most of the chopped leaves and the peppers, and cook for a minute or two more. Add the tomatoes with their liquid and the stock. Bring to a simmer and cook gently for about 20 minutes.

3 | Add the dumplings to the soup about halfway through the cooking time. At the end of the cooking time, when the dumplings are cooked, stir the okra into the soup and turn off the heat. Adjust the seasoning to taste.

4 | Put 2-3 *kubba* in the bottom of each bowl, pour the soup over and garnish with the reserved celery leaves.

Okra

(Hibiscus esculenta)

This unique vegetable, a member of the mallow, or *hibiscus*, family, originated in Africa and still grows wild in Ethiopia. It is the elongated edible pod that results from the brilliant red and yellow blooms. *Bamia* in Arabic, *bhindi* in India and "ladies' fingers" in English (okra is a corruption of an African name), few vegetables excite such different responses.

The sticky juices inside the pod, useful in cooking as a thickener, turn many people off. We always keep the pods whole and fry them first to reduce this "goopiness". Other people soak them for a few hours in water acidulated with lemon juice or vinegar. Some people make the mistake of thinking that the longer you cook okra the less sticky it will seem, but without either preliminary frying or soaking it just goes on getting stickier as you cook it.

Like us, though, many people love okra's delicate taste and lovely texture – described variously as a cross between aubergine and asparagus, or even green beans and gooseberries. Okra was served to us as kids in *bamia cutta* (see opposite) or in dryish sour curries. We still love it – even more so now that we have learned that the sticky juices help soothe irritated digestive tracts.

Perhaps due to the proliferation of Indian restaurants and markets, okra has recently become more widely available in Britain. Don't buy pods that are too large (more than about 8cm/3¼in), as this means they have been harvested too late and will be tough, fibrous and indigestible. Look for firmness, a rich green skin and no discoloration. Okra goes well with tomatoes and onions, and souring agents such as lemon juice and tamarind, as well as both ground coriander and its fresh leaves. Don't cook okra in utensils made of reactive metals such as tin, or pan and vegetable will go a very unappetizing colour!

Sweetcorn Chowder

This tasty soup can be varied hugely according to what vegetables are available – for example, use potatoes, turnips or parsnips instead of artichokes, and/or sweet potatoes instead of squash.

SERVES 4

3 corn cobs
3 tbsp vegetable oil
1 large chilli, seeded and finely
  chopped
handful of thyme leaves, chopped
1 large onion, finely chopped
3 garlic cloves, finely chopped
1 small leek, finely chopped
2 celery stalks, diced, (reserving
  any leaves)
200g (7oz) peeled and seeded
  butternut squash, diced

150g (5½oz) Jerusalem artichokes,
  diced
2 tsp sugar
1 litre (1¾ pints) vegetable stock
  (page 40)
salt and black pepper
small handful of coriander
  leaves, chopped
juice of ½ lime
single cream (optional)

1 | Brush the corn cobs with a little of the vegetable oil and colour them in a hot, dry frying pan for 5-6 minutes, until nicely browned all over.

2 | When the cobs are cool enough to handle, stand each one on its end on a chopping board (or in a large bowl steadied on a damp cloth to catch all the kernels) and remove the kernels by cutting down all around the edge of the core with a sharp, heavy knife.

3 | Heat the remaining oil in a large heavy-based pot over a moderate heat and cook the chilli, thyme, onion, garlic, leek and celery, stirring frequently, until softened.

4 | Add the squash, corn kernels and artichokes with the sugar and cook gently, stirring frequently, for about 15 minutes, until everything is nicely caramelized, breaking down and just beginning to catch on the bottom of the pan.

5 | Add the stock, bring to a rapid simmer, and cook for about 10-15 minutes until slightly reduced. Season to taste.

6 | With a stick blender, partially purée the soup until it is creamy but still has a lot of texture. (If your pan is deep, the best way to do this is to hold the stick blender at a slight angle, as this circulates the contents of the soup nicely.)

7 | Just before serving, stir in the coriander and squeeze in a little lime juice to taste. If you like, you can add some single cream or just swirl some into each bowl of soup.

Spicy Apple, Fennel and Sweet Potato Soup

The creation of this soup came from an urge to have a sweet soup that was also pretty spicy.

SERVES 4

2 tbsp vegetable oil
1 red chilli, seeded and
 finely chopped
4 cardamom pods, crushed
2 tsp each of ground turmeric,
 cinnamon and cumin
1 tsp ground coriander
1-2 tbsp garam masala
1 tbsp black mustard seeds
1 large onion, finely chopped

large chunk of fresh root ginger,
 finely chopped or grated
3-4 garlic cloves, finely chopped
1 fennel bulb, cored and diced
2 sweet potatoes, peeled
 and diced
2-3 Jerusalem artichokes, diced
2-3 parsnips, peeled and diced
about 1.25 litres (2 pints)
 vegetable stock (see page 40)

2 firm eating apples, such as Granny
 Smiths, peeled, cored and cut into
 chunks
salt and black pepper
1-2 tbsp sugar
handful of coriander leaves, chopped
1 pickled lemon (see page 112),
 finely chopped, with 1 tbsp of the
 pickling liquid
125g (4oz) runny yoghurt

1 | Heat the oil in a large wok or frying pan and stir-fry the chilli and all the spices until they give off their aromas. Add the onion, ginger and garlic and stir-fry until they soften.

2 | Add the vegetables and turn to coat in the oil and flavourings for 2-3 minutes. Add the stock, bring to the boil, then simmer gently for 20-25 minutes, until they are tender. Half way through that time, add the apples.

3 | Using a stick blender, reduce the contents of the pan to a purée. Season to taste with salt and pepper and add sugar to taste to bring out the natural sweetness of the vegetables. Stir in the chopped coriander.

4 | Mix the chopped pickled lemon and its liquid into the yoghurt and swirl this into each bowl of soup to serve.

Jerusalem Artichoke Soup

with Trompettes-des-Morts and Truffle Oil

We created this dish for our first Mushroom Fest and, like the festival, it went down well. The idea was to use mushrooms in unusual ways as well as making the most of their individual flavours. The delicacy of the *trompettes* goes well with that of the truffle oil.

SERVES 4

1kg (2¼lb) Jerusalem artichokes, halved
2-3 tbsp olive oil, plus more for brushing
salt and white pepper

2 large knobs butter
2 leeks, trimmed and finely chopped
2 tbsp chopped rosemary
1 fennel bulb, core removed, finely chopped

1 potato, finely diced
about 500ml (18fl oz) vegetable stock (page 40)
12-16 trompettes-des-morts
few drops of truffle oil

1 | Preheat the oven to 200°C/400°F/gas mark 6. Brush the artichokes with oil and season well with salt and white pepper, then roast for about 30 minutes.

2 | Heat the remaining oil and half the butter in a large heavy-based pan and sauté the leeks until soft. Stir in the rosemary and fennel and sweat gently for 2-3 minutes. Add the artichokes and potato and cook gently for 4-5 minutes more.

3 | Pour in the stock, bring to the boil and simmer gently for 30 minutes, until all the vegetables are tender.

4 | Purée the soup in a blender or with a stick blender (most domestic food processors aren't quite up to this job). Bring back to the heat and adjust the seasoning if necessary.

5 | While the soup is reheating, sauté the mushrooms in the remaining butter with a little drop of oil to prevent it burning in a very hot pan until nicely crisped on the outside.

6 | To serve, float the mushrooms on top of each bowl of soup and finish with a few drops of the truffle oil.

Thai-inspired Butternut Squash and Fennel Soup

You could use the Thai red curry paste (page 183) to flavour the soup, but we prefer the fresher lighter flavours of the ingredients here.

SERVES 4

2 tbsp sesame oil

dash of olive oil

2-3 banana shallots, chopped

1 lemongrass stalk, outer leaves discarded, chopped

2-3 garlic cloves, chopped

large chunk of fresh root ginger, coarsely chopped

700g (1lb 9oz) peeled butternut squash (1 good-sized squash), seeded and coarsely chopped

2 fennel bulbs, cored and coarsely chopped

2-3 celery stalks, coarsely chopped

1 recipe quantity Thai stock (see page 35)

large handful of coriander leaves, chopped

handful of basil, preferably Thai

lime juice, to finish

soy sauce, to taste

1 | Heat the oils in a large heavy-based pan, add the shallots and sweat until softened. Add the lemongrass, garlic and ginger and continue to cook gently, stirring for 3-4 minutes. Add the vegetables and cook slowly for 10 minutes more, stirring from time to time, until the vegetables slightly caramelize.

2 | Add the stock, bring to the boil and simmer for 20-25 minutes until everything is tender.

3 | Stir in the coriander and basil, and blend to a purée with a stick blender. Finish with a squeeze of lime juice and soy sauce to taste.

Watercress, Wild Garlic and Rocket Soup

We created this wonderfully simple soup to celebrate the fresh green flavours of the early English summer after spending some pleasant weekends in Wiltshire. If you can't lay your hands on wild garlic leaves, just add a couple of finely chopped garlic cloves with the onion.

SERVES 4

1 tbsp vegetable oil
25g (1oz) butter
2 onions, finely chopped
2 sprigs rosemary
450g (1lb) Jerusalem artichokes,
  potatoes or parsnips, diced
salt and black pepper

1 litre (1¾ pints) vegetable
  stock (page 40)
2 large bunches watercress
about 10 wild garlic leaves
good handful of rocket
juice of ½ lemon
soured cream, to serve (optional)

1 | Heat the oil and butter in a large heavy-based pan and sweat the onions with the rosemary until the onions are softened. Add the root vegetable, season to taste and stir to coat for a minute or so.

2 | Add the stock, bring to a simmer and cook gently for about 30 minutes until the root vegetables is soft.

3 | With a stick blender, purée the soup until it is creamy but still has a bit of texture. (If your pan is deep, the best way to do this is to hold the stick blender at a slight angle, as this circulates the contents of the soup nicely.) Add the greens and blend them well into the puréed soup to produce a velvety texture.

4 | Finish with a squeeze of lemon juice and serve swirled with soured cream if you like.

Thom Yam
(Traditional Thai hot-and-sour soup)

We like to eat this soup with rice, but it is more usually served with noodles. For a special version of the soup, we sometimes replace the noodles with ravioli stuffed with a *duxelles* of shiitake mushrooms. If you have some of our Thai red curry paste (page 183), use that to make a stock in place of the herbs and spices – just add 2 tbsp of water with the vegetables.

SERVES 4

55g (2oz) fresh egg noodles
55g (2oz) each of carrots and mange touts, cut into julienne strips
8 baby sweetcorn, quartered lengthways
1 red pepper, seeded and excess inner flesh removed, cut into strips
3-4 tbsp soy sauce
juice of 1 lime

toasted black and white mustard seeds and coriander leaves

THAI STOCK
2 tbsp sesame oil
2 Thai shallots or 1 large onion
4 celery stalks (or, if you have a good celery head, just use the base)
1 red pepper, seeded (optional)

2-3 tomatoes
1 carrot
5cm (2in) chunk each of fresh root ginger and galangal
3-4 red chillies
5-6 garlic cloves
12 lime leaves
6 lemongrass stalks
handful of coriander stalks

1 | To make the stock, heat the oil in a large heavy-based pan and, without peeling the vegetables or aromatics, roughly chop them all and stir them into the pan as they are ready.

2 | Half-fill the pan with water and bring to the boil. Reduce the heat and simmer gently for about 30 minutes.

3 | Cook the noodles according to packet instructions, drain in a colander and refresh under cold running water until quite cold. Set aside.

4 | Pass the cooked stock through a sieve, return it to the pan and bring back to the boil. Stir in the fresh vegetables and cook for about 1 minute.

5 | Stir in the noodles to warm through and season to taste with soy sauce and lime juice to serve. Garnish with toasted mustard seeds and whole coriander leaves.

Quick Soups

As you can readily see in this chapter, there is nothing magic or complicated about making good vegetarian soups, and they can be among the quickest, easiest and most satisfying dishes that you can make at home.

A good stock (page 40) is obviously the biggest necessity and, if you don't have any in the pot or in the freezer, there are many excellent storecupboard substitutes. Some stock cubes (even some "fresh" stock now being sold in supermarkets) are oversalted and chemical-tasting – but Marigold vegetable bouillon powder, long a "foodie secret", is now widely available.

When preparing an Oriental noodle soup, we recommend sachets of miso stock powder, to be found in health-food and whole-food shops as well as Asian stores. There are several varieties, some flavoured with mushrooms, which Adrian favours. Make a stock from one of these, add a handful or two of mange touts, beansprouts and chopped spring onions with some egg noodles, flavour with soy sauce and you can have the most delicious and fairly authentic of soups in less than five minutes.

To prepare yourself an instant *laksa*, use one or two cubes of our Thai red curry paste (page 183), which you have cleverly prepared in bulk and frozen in ice-cube trays (if you haven't exercised that much forethought, use a couple of spoonfuls of one of the several good ready-prepared curry pastes on sale). Cook the paste in a large pan until aromatic, add a can of coconut milk, a litre (1¾ pints) of stock, a generous handful of cubed tofu, a packet of beansprouts, lots of sliced mushrooms, some chopped spring onions and some rice vermicelli. Bring to a simmer and season with soy sauce.

Using a stick blender can facilitate putting together wonderful no-cook soups – try whizzing lovely ripe vine tomatoes with cream or yoghurt and some suitable herbs such as chervil or basil, or blending some ready-cooked beetroot (not vinegared) with stock, spring onions, coriander and mint for a quick cutta (page 20); or make the guacamole on page 208 and thin down with stock for an avocado soup. All of these are great chilled or warmed up.

In fact, many of the items in our Pestos and All That Jazz chapter can be pressed into service to this end. Puréed roasted garlic (page 212) can add depth to any soups, and a little pickled lemon (page 112) can bring a host of soups to life.

For something really warming in a hurry, make a quick version of our Glastonbury-wowing spinach and tomato dhal (page 39): blend a cooked canned pulse such as lentils, haricots or chickpeas with a can of chopped tomatoes, some fresh or frozen spinach and a little stock if you have it, then flavour with whichever spices you have to hand (curry powder gives quite nice results).

a quick spinach and tomato dhal

Pumpkin Soup

with Basil Pesto Ravioli

Adrian confesses that one evening he made a large batch of pumpkin soup that was perfectly nice but just a bit boring, so he came up with this idea of adding a big splash of flavour to the soup by means of a raviolo filled with pesto.

SERVES 4

1 tbsp olive oil
good knob of butter
good sprig each of rosemary
and thyme
1 small onion, finely chopped
3-4 garlic cloves, finely chopped
1 leek, trimmed and chopped

4-5 celery stalks, roughly chopped
500g (18oz) peeled and seeded
pumpkin or squash, roughly
chopped
about 1.5 litres (2¾ pints) vegetable
stock (page 40)
salt and black pepper

BASIL PESTO RAVIOLI

200g (7oz) plain flour or Italian
"00" (doppio zero) flour
1 egg, plus 1 extra egg yolk
pinch of salt
splash of oil
3 tbsp basil pesto (see page 178)

1 | Well ahead, make the basil pesto ravioli: mix the flour, whole egg, salt and oil in a blender, and then bring together with some cold water (2-3 spoonfuls at the most) to form a coherent dough. Knead for about 10 minutes until smooth, then wrap in foil or plastic wrap and leave to rest in the fridge for about 1 hour.

2 | Roll the rested pasta dough to the thickness of a thin coin and cut out eight 5cm (2in) circles with a pastry cutter. Put a teaspoonful of pesto in the centre of each, moisten edges with beaten egg yolk and fold over in half. Pinch all round to seal into nice half-moon shapes. Leave to dry for 1 hour.

3 | Heat the oil and butter in a large heavy-based pan and stir in the herbs. Add the onion, garlic and leek, and sweat gently for about 2-3 minutes until softened. Toss in the celery and squash, turn to coat it all and cook for 2 minutes over a fairly high heat.

4 | Add the stock with seasoning to taste (not too heavy, you want a fairly muted background to the punch of the basil), bring to the boil and simmer gently for 30 minutes, until the vegetables are soft.

5 | With a stick blender, purée the soup until it is creamy but still has a bit of texture. (If your pan is nice and deep, the best way to do this is to hold the stick blender at a slight angle as this circulates the content of the soup nicely.)

6 | Meanwhile, blanch the ravioli in salted boiling water for 1 minute. Float two of the drained ravioli on top of each bowl of soup to serve.

Spinach and Tomato Dhal

"Dhal" or "dal" is the Indian term for a wide range of pulses and the dishes made from them, generally soupy stews. One of our first ventures into catering was arriving at the Glastonbury Festival with two big pots of this soup, a spirit burner, some jerry cans and little else. It was all a bit like something on the streets of Calcutta.

SERVES 4

200g (7oz) red lentils or yellow
   split peas
1 tbsp panch phoran
2 tbsp olive oil
1 tbsp each of ground cumin,
   coriander and turmeric
1 tsp each of ground cloves
   and cinnamon
1 small onion, finely chopped
4 garlic cloves, finely chopped

3 tomatoes, blanched, skinned
   and diced (or 1 x 400g can chopped
   tomatoes)
1 tsp tomato purée
about 200g (7oz) spinach leaves,
   shredded
handful of chopped coriander
salt and black pepper
squeeze of lemon juice, to finish

1 | Put the lentils in a large pan and add 1.5 litres (2¾ pints) cold water. Bring to the boil, then simmer for 15-20 minutes, until just tender.

2 | Toast the panch phoran seeds in a dry wok or large frying pan until they pop. Add the oil, heat through and stir-fry all the spices until aromatic. Add the onion and garlic, and sweat until softened.

3 | Add the contents of the lentil pan, the tomatoes and the tomato purée, and cook for 15 minutes.

4 | Finish the dhal by stirring in the spinach and coriander, seasoning to taste and adding a little lemon juice.

Basic Vegetable Stock

Never throw away your vegetable and herb trimmings, as they can all help make a richly flavoured stock. Either have a steady stockpot going to which you add all your trimmings (remembering to boil it up each day to keep it sweet), or make a large batch, strain and reduce it down by about two-thirds, then freeze in ice-cube trays. You can then use just one cube for a quick solo supper, etc.

MAKES 1.5 LITRES (2¾ PINTS)
2 carrots, roughly chopped
3 celery stalks (with any leaves), roughly chopped
2 bay leaves
small handful of black peppercorns
1 large onion, quartered
few parsley stalks or any herb trimmings (leaves, stalks and washed roots)

1 | Put everything in a large pot with about 1.75 litres (3 pints) of cold water, or enough to cover generously. Bring to a simmer, skim off any scum and continue to simmer gently for about 30 minutes.

2 | Sieve and use to allow to cool, or see above.

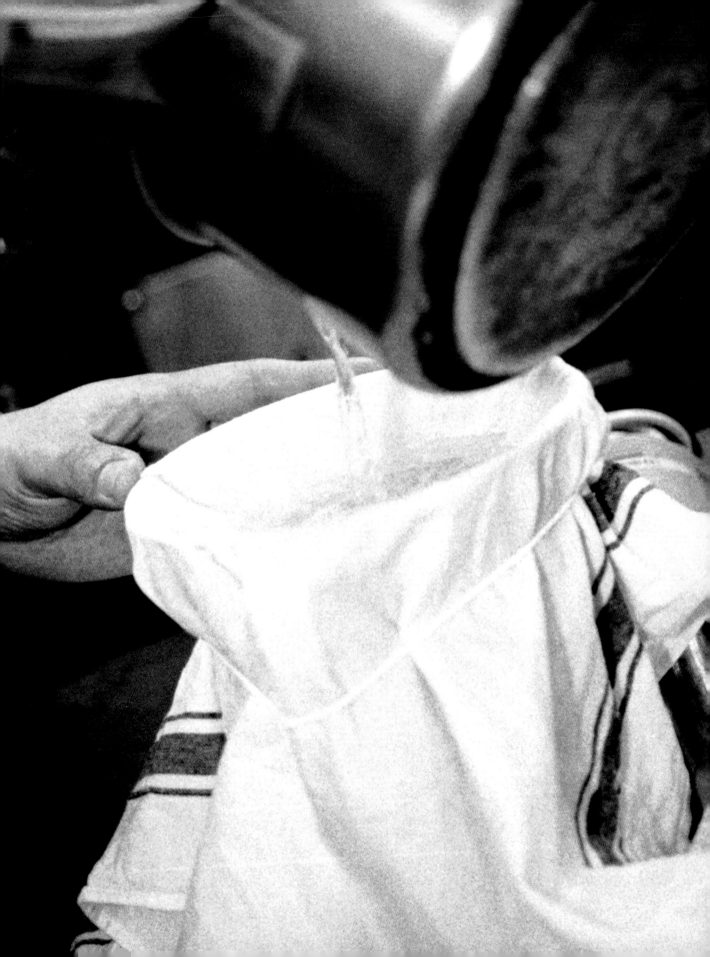

Starters and Snacks

We are great proponents of starters, and we like the idea of meals that are made up of lots of little courses, so we often eat that way at home, in our restaurants and when eating out in other places. The idea behind starters is that they are light, sharpen the palate and get the juices flowing – so why shouldn't that apply to every stage of the meal?

As you can see from much of what we say in this book, little highly flavoured snacks are very much part of both our Indo-Iraqi and our family traditions. Even our special meals for get-togethers tend to be spreads of little things, so you can pick at what you fancy. The little dishes served as appetizers then go on to act as side dishes alongside the main course(s).

As a bonus, therefore, many of the dishes in this chapter, such as the dumplings, sushi, wontons, spring rolls, etc, also make great party food, although you might have to make them slightly smaller or cut them into bite-sized pieces.

Fortunately for our menus, it is not just the Indo-Iraqi tradition that is inclined to such dishes; both Oriental and Mediterranean food are rich in these little tasty gems, so we have been able to build starters and snacks into one of our strongest areas.

Japanese Spring Rolls
with Miso Dressing

We created this for the restaurant as a healthy light dish for the summer that isn't oily but is full of flavour.

SERVES 4

2 courgettes
1 large aubergine
55g (2oz) fresh shiitake mushrooms
salt
1 red and 1 yellow pepper
sesame oil
36-48 large spinach leaves (if they are big enough you might only need 12), veins removed
pickled pink ginger, to serve

MISO DRESSING
1 tbsp barley miso
1 red chilli, seeded and thinly sliced
100ml (3½fl oz) light soy sauce
½ tbsp finely chopped fresh root ginger
1 tbsp muscovado sugar
juice of 1 lime
50ml (2fl oz) sesame oil

1 | Cut the courgettes, aubergine and mushrooms lengthways into thin strips about 5cm (2in) long. Salt the aubergine and set aside for 30 minutes, then rinse thoroughly and pat dry. If roasting the vegetables, preheat the oven to 190°C/375°F/gas mark 5 or preheat a barbecue or (nearer the time) a griddle pan.

2 | Brush the sliced vegetables and the peppers with sesame oil and char-grill for 2-3 minutes on each side or roast for 10-15 minutes, until softened and nicely coloured. When cool enough to handle, cut the peppers in half, scoop out the seeds and cut into strips like the other vegetables.

3 | While the vegetables are cooking, blanch the spinach leaves for an instant only in boiling water, refresh in cold water and drain well.

4 | Arrange two to three (depending on size – you might only need one if large enough) of the blanched spinach leaves overlapping in the shape of a larger leaf and roll them with a rolling pin to flatten them and bond them together. Arrange about one-twelfth of the vegetable strips in layers across the spinach leaves, then roll up the leave(s) from the 'stem' ends. (For technique see pages 48-49.)

5 | In a bowl, mix together all the ingredients for the miso dressing. Drizzle the dressing over the spinach rolls and serve with the pickled pink ginger.

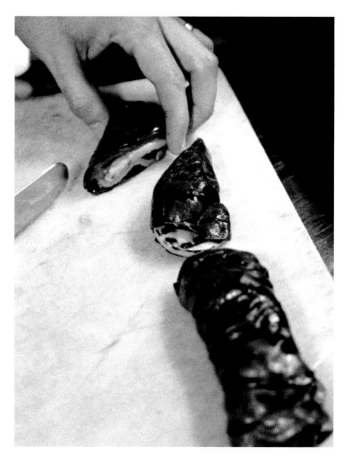

Spring Rolls

The basic idea of the spring roll – that familiar little Chinese starter – appealed to us as a way of presenting mixtures of raw or cooked vegetables, as they usually also give the opportunity of producing an exciting contrast in tastes and textures both within the filling and between the filling and the outer casing. The classic spring roll (so-called as they were traditionally served at Chinese New Year) usually consists of a tasty minced mixture and fresh beansprouts within a crunchy fried pastry wrapper.

One of the spring roll ideas that we have tried with considerable success is replacing the fried pastry wrappers with blanched spinach leaves (see the recipe on page 46). In these, the contrast is between the crunchy vegetables inside and the silky spinach exterior. A more traditional treatment, using spring roll wrappers or wonton skins, can be seen in our Shiitake Wontons recipe on page 55.

To make our spinach spring rolls:

1 | Arrange two to three (depending on size – you might only need one if large enough) of the blanched spinach leaves overlapping in the shape of a larger leaf and roll them with a rolling pin to flatten them and bond them together.

2 | Arrange the vegetable fillings in layers across the spinach leaves.

3&4 | Roll up the spinach leave(s) from the "stem" ends.

5 | Slice the cylinder produced across at an angle to produce attractively shaped pieces.

If you are making classic wontons like the Shiitake Wontons on page 55:

Lay each spring roll wrapper or wonton skin (make sure you buy the type of wonton skins meant for frying rather than those produced for steaming) in front of you and place a heaped spoonful of the mixture in its centre. Brush the edges of the skin with egg or cornflour paste. Bring up two opposing corners, followed by the other two corners, pinch along the edges and twist the top to seal.

Heat groundnut oil for deep-frying in the wok or a deep frying pan or a deep-fat fryer and fry the spring rolls or wontons in batches of three to four at a time, for about 2-3 minutes each, until crisp and golden brown all over. Drain on kitchen paper.

Nori Rolls

This is Adrian's version of a varied vegetarian sushi.

SERVES 8
**2½ cups Japanese fancy rice or other
  short-grained rice**
5 tbsp rice vinegar
**2½ tbsp *mirin* (Japanese sweet
  rice wine)**
1 tbsp sugar
8 sheets ready-toasted *nori* seaweed
***wasabi* (optional)**

MARINATED SHIITAKE FILLING
about 6 shiitake mushrooms, sliced
2 tbsp sesame oil
2 tbsp soy sauce
1 tbsp *mirin*

**PICKLED CARROT AND
RADISH FILLING**
1 small carrot, in julienne strips
½ mooli radish, in julienne strips
4 tbsp soy sauce
2 tbsp *mirin*

AVOCADO AND WASABI FILLING
**1 small avocado, halved, stoned,
  peeled and in julienne strips**
**1 tbsp *wasabi*, loosened with a little
  water**

CUCUMBER AND WASABI FILLING
**¼ cucumber, halved lengthwise,
  seeded and in julienne strips**

**1 tbsp *wasabi*, loosened with a little
  water**

RED PEPPER FILLING
**1 red pepper, halved, seeded and
  in julienne strips**
4 tbsp toasted sesame seeds

TO SERVE
pickled pink ginger
wasabi
**more carrot strips and crescents of
  mooli, plus some *wakame* seaweed
  (optional) dressed in rice vinegar
  soy sauce**

1 | Rinse the rice in a sieve under cold running water for about 30 minutes, occasionally rubbing the grains between the fingers.

2 | Bring 600ml (1 pint) water to the boil in a large pan. Add the rice, bring back to the boil and stir. Cover with a tea-towel, then the pan lid, and place over the gentlest of heats for 10 minutes. Take off the heat and leave undisturbed for another 10 minutes. Remove the lid and tea-towel and stir in the rice vinegar, *mirin* and sugar. If you have the patience, fan the rice to cool it down quickly.

3 | Make the marinated shiitake filling by sautéing the mushroom slices in the sesame oil until softened, then tip into a bowl. Dress with the soy sauce and *mirin*, and leave to cool.

4 | Make the pickled carrot and radish filling by dressing the carrot and mooli strips with the soy sauce and *mirin*.

5 | Make the avocado and *wasabi* and cucumber and *wasabi* fillings by dressing the strips of avocado and cucumber respectively with the diluted *wasabi*.

6 | Lay a sheet of the *nori* out in front of you and spoon one-tenth of the rice over the half of it closest to you. If you like, spread a line of *wasabi* across the middle of the rice. Arrange half of one of the fillings evenly down that line. Lift the nearer end of the nori and roll it up tightly around the filling to make a neat cylinder. Seal the final outer edge of *nori* to the cylinder by dampening it slightly. Repeat with the other sheets of *nori* and the remaining fillings except the red pepper.

7 | To make the red pepper rolls, don't use any *nori*, simply arrange a piece of clingfilm larger than a sheet of *nori* on the work surface and arrange half the rice on it as you did on the *nori*, then arrange the red pepper strips as you did the other fillings. Roll up tightly to make a neat cylinder again, then remove the clingfilm and press the sesame seeds into the rice evenly all over. Do this again with the remaining rice, pepper strips and sesame seeds.

8 | Slice each roll across into four pieces, then cut each of those pieces at an angle into two. Arrange a piece with each filling on each plate, and surround with little piles of pickled pink ginger, *wasabi* and carrot and *mooli* strips and *wakame* seaweed if you have it. Give each person a small shallow bowl of soy sauce.

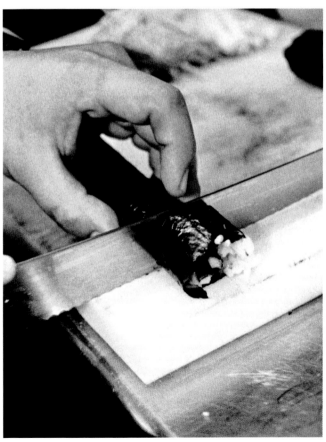

Sushi

Sushi is wonderfully versatile. It can be served as a snack, as party finger food, or even as a full meal – and it allows you to showcase the flavours of lots of different vegetables. Vegetable sushi has been served alongside the fish types for centuries, so there is lots of traditional inspiration.

Getting the rice right is obviously a large part of the secret of good sushi. We use imported Japanese rice selected especially for the purpose, but you can use any short-grained glutinous (i.e. sticky) rice. Traditionally the boiled rice is mixed with just rice vinegar to make the basic sushi *meshi*, as it is known, but we also add a little *mirin* (Japanese sweet rice wine) and a bit of sugar to enhance the sweetness of the rice.

Even though you are aiming for stickiness, it is a good idea first to rinse the rice in a sieve under cold running water for about 30 minutes. The rice is then stirred into boiling unsalted water, brought back to a simmer, covered with a tea-towel and the pan lid, then cooked over the gentlest of heats until just tender (about 10 minutes). It is then taken off the heat and left undisturbed for 10 minutes. The lid and towel are removed and the rice vinegar, *mirin* and sugar stirred in. If you have the patience, fan the rice to cool it down quickly –

in Japan people are hired just to perform this important function.

To make the sushi:

1 | Lay a sheet of toasted *nori* out in front of you on top of a sushi mat (some clingfilm baking paper will work if you haven't got any of these) and spoon some the rice over the half of if closest to you.

2 | If you like, spread a line of *wasabi* across the middle of the rice.

3 | Arrange some of the filling evenly down that line.

4&5 | Lift the nearer end of the *nori*.

6 | Roll it up tightly around the filling to make a neat cylinder. Seal the final outer edge of the *nori* to the cylinder by dampening it slightly.

7 | Trim off the ends. and slice each roll across at angles into four pieces, then cut each of those pieces at an angle into two. Serve surrounded with little piles of the traditional accompaniments of pickled pink ginger, *wasabi* and carrot and *mooli* strips. Give each person a small shallow bowl of soy sauce.

Shiitake Wontons

Make sure you buy the type of wonton skins meant for frying, rather than those produced for steaming. If you can't get rice vinegar for the dipping sauce, or if it is prohibitively expensive, just use all white wine vinegar.

SERVES 4

1 tbsp each of sesame and groundnut oil
1 onion, finely chopped
300g (10½oz) shiitake mushrooms, diced
2 fat garlic cloves, finely chopped
1 small red chilli, seeded and finely chopped
1cm (½in) piece fresh root ginger, finely chopped
splash of soy sauce
handful of coriander leaves, chopped

juice of 1 lime
12 wonton skins
egg or cornflour and water paste, to seal
groundnut oil, for deep-frying

DIPPING SAUCE
200ml (7fl oz) rice vinegar
dash of white wine vinegar
2 red chillies, seeded and finely chopped
1 lime leaf

1 lemongrass stalk, sliced
small knob of fresh root ginger, finely chopped
sugar or honey to taste

VEGETABLE SALAD
2 carrots, scrubbed
handful of mange tout, trimmed
2 red peppers, seeded
drizzle of sesame oil
juice of 1 lime

1 | Make the dipping sauce well ahead by mixing all the ingredients together, to allow the flavours to get friendly.

2 | Heat the oils in a wok and, when good and hot, add the onion and stir-fry over a medium heat until softened. Add the mushrooms, garlic, chilli and ginger, and stir-fry until the mushrooms soften. Stir in the soy sauce and finish with the coriander and lime juice.

3 | Pulse the contents of the wok in a blender until it makes a rough mixture. Leave to cool.

4 | To prepare the salad, cut all the vegetables into julienne strips and toss them together with the remaining ingredients. Set aside.

5 | Lay each wonton skin in front of you and place a heaped spoonful of the mixture in its centre. Brush the edges of the skin with egg or cornflour paste. Bring up two opposing corners, followed by the other two corners, pinch along the edges and twist the top to seal.

6 | Heat the groundnut oil for deep-frying in the wok or a deep frying pan or a deep-fat fryer and fry the wontons in batches of three or four at a time, for about 2-3 minutes each, until crisp and golden brown all over. Drain on kitchen paper.

7 | Pile some of the salad in the centre of four plates and arrange three wontons on each. Serve the dipping sauce in small bowls.

Ajja

This fresh, slightly souffléed, omelette was a popular Sunday breakfast dish in our family, but it makes an excellent snack at any time of the day, especially if served with a mixed salad as here. The true joy of this ajja (the word really means just omelette) is the successful and refreshing combination of the mint, coriander and chilli.

SERVES 2

3 eggs
1 small red chilli, seeded
  and finely chopped
small handful of coriander
  leaves, chopped
small handful of mint
  leaves, chopped

salt and black pepper
a little butter
1 tbsp vegetable oil
1 or 2 pitta breads, to serve
mixed salad, to serve (optional)

1 | Separate the eggs into two bowls. Beat the yolks lightly and mix in the chilli and herbs with seasonings to taste (remembering they will have to season the egg white too).

2 | Beat the egg whites until foamy. Add a spoonful to the egg yolk mixture to loosen it and then carefully stir in the rest of the egg whites with as few strokes as possible, so as not to lose too much of the beaten-in air.

3 | Heat the butter and oil together in an omelette or pancake pan and swirl to coat the base. When fairly hot, pour in the mixture, turn the heat down to low-to-medium and cook until the edges of the *ajja* come away from the sides of the pan. Turn over and cook the other side for a minute or so, no more.

4 | While the eggs are cooking, cut the breads in half and toast lightly if you want. Serve the *ajja* cut into wedges and popped into the bread cavities, accompanied by a side salad if you like.

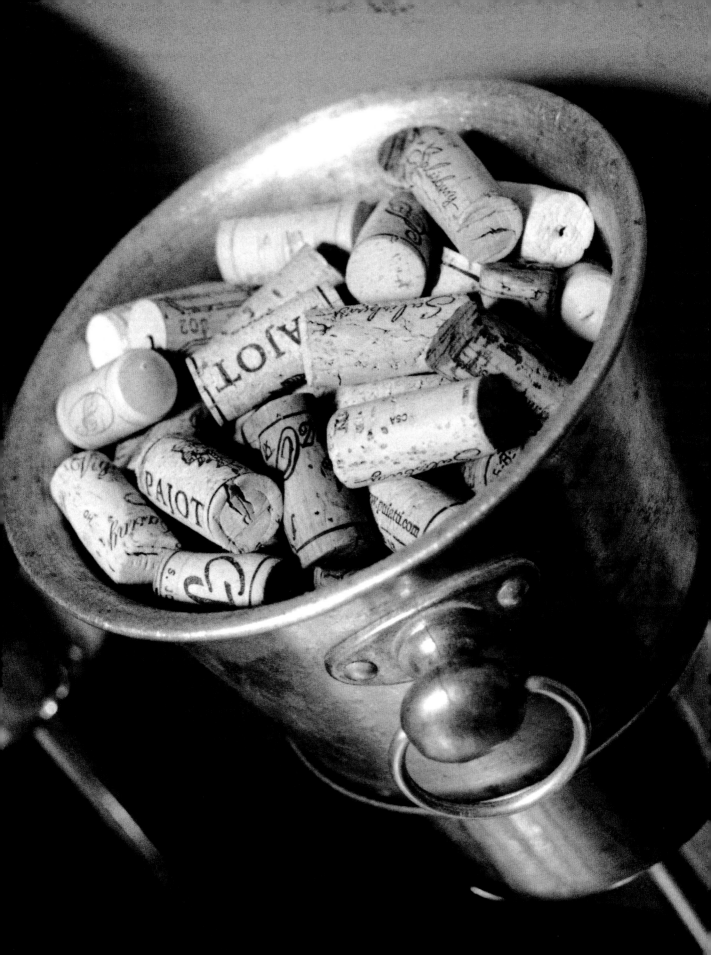

Plantain Fritters

These little delights were initially inspired by traditional *kubba* (pages 22-23). The plaintain is one of those underused vegetables that people see in West Indian markets but don't know how to use.

SERVES 4

3-4 small plantains
300g (10½oz) sweet potatoes
  (preferably orange-fleshed)
vegetable oil, for deep-frying
good handful of salad greens, to serve
chilli coulis (page 182), to serve
chive stalks, to serve

STUFFING
2 tbsp sultanas or dates
1 tbsp each of olive oil and
  vegetable oil

1 large red chilli, seeded and
  finely chopped
3 garlic cloves, finely chopped
5cm (2in) fresh root ginger, grated
5-6 shallots or 2 banana shallots,
  finely chopped
1 small carrot, grated
2 tsp sugar
juice of 1 lime
2 tbsp toasted pine nuts
handful each of mint and
  coriander leaves, chopped

SWEET CREAM CHILLI SAUCE
touch of olive oil
1 large red chilli, seeded and
  finely chopped
2 small shallots, finely chopped
½ garlic clove, finely chopped
1 tbsp granulated sugar
1 tbsp *mirin* (Japanese sweet
  rice wine)
250ml (9fl oz) double cream

1 | Well ahead, make the stuffing. Soak the sultanas in warm water for 10 minutes, then drain and roughly chop. Heat the oils in a large frying pan or wok and cook the chilli for 30 seconds, then stir in the garlic, ginger and shallots and cook gently for about 5-10 minutes. Add the carrot and cook for 6-7 minutes more, until this is soft. (If the mixture catches, stir in a few drops of water; don't worry as a little charring adds to the flavour.) Stir in the sugar until dissolved, then stir in the lime juice, pine nuts, sultanas or dates and herbs. Leave to sit for 3-4 hours to let the flavours develop.

2 | To make the fritters, preheat the oven to 220°C/425°F/gas mark 7 and roast the plantains and sweet potatoes in their skins for about 30 minutes, until the plantain skins split and the flesh inside has darkened.

3 | When cool enough to handle, remove the skins from the plantains and rinse them while still warm as this helps them mash more easily. Peel off the sweet potato skin. Mash the vegetables, ideally using a *mouli-légumes*. Mix thoroughly.

4 | Roll the mixture into 12-16 ping-pong-sized balls. There are two ways of stuffing the fritters: either push a thumb deep into a ball and pile the stuffing into the hole, then push in the edges around the hole to seal it; or make them *kubba* fashion (see pages 62-63) by flattening the ball out, placing a spoonful of the stuffing in the centre, folding the mixture around the stuffing and rolling it back into a sealed ball. The *kubba* method lets you get more stuffing into the fritter (and makes a bigger fritter). Chill the fritters for at least 30 minutes.

5 | For the sauce, heat the oil in a small frying pan and sauté the chilli briefly, then add the shallots and garlic and sauté for 1-2 minutes more. Stir in the sugar, *mirin* and cream, bring to just below the boil, still stirring, and take off the heat. Sieve and keep warm.

6 | To cook the fritters, heat 3cm (1¼in) of vegetable oil in a wok or large frying pan until almost smoking and cook the fritters in two to three batches, turning them so they cook evenly, for 2-3 minutes until golden. Remove with a slotted spoon and drain on kitchen paper. Keep warm while you cook the rest in the same way.

7 | To serve, arrange three to four fritters in the middle of each plate on green salad leaves, pour the cream sauce around, speckle the plate with chilli coulis and scatter over some chives stalks.

1 | 2 | 3
4 | 5 | 6
    | 7

Fritters

Fritters were a regular part of our Mum's everyday cooking. Not only did everyone love these little crisp nuggets with a deliciously soft tasty filling – they were sort of our fish and chips – but they were an excellent way of using up leftovers. In the restaurant we have found them an invaluable way of bringing a wide range of added flavours and fresh textures to our vegetable dishes.

As you can see from the fritter recipes in this book, sometimes we stuff them, but often we just mix the extra flavouring ingredients into the base mixture – be it potato, sweet potato, plantain, green banana or couscous – before rolling it into balls. The advantage of doing it this way is that you can make the fritters smaller, to give you excellent one- or two-bite party food.

However, nothing beats that lovely surprise when you bite into a fritter through the crisp exterior and then the soft base mix into a hidden nugget of flavoursome delight. There are two ways of stuffing the fritters. For the first method:

1 | Push a thumb deep into a ping-pong-sized ball of base mixture.
2 | Pile the filling into the hole.
3 | Push the edges around the hole to seal it.
The *kubba* method (see pages 22-23) has the advantage of allowing you to get more stuffing into the fritter (and makes a slightly bigger fritter). For this method:

4 | Flatten the ball out making a depression in its centre.
5 | Place a spoonful of the stuffing in the hole.
6 | Fold the mixture up and around the stuffing and roll it back into a sealed ball.
7 |. Once all the fritters are stuffed, chill them for at least 30 minutes before cooking. The secret of good deep-frying is to get the oil good and hot – almost smoking – and to cook only small batches at a time, so the temperature of the oil doesn't drop too much. This way the food absorbs remarkably little oil, especially if you drain well on kitchen paper as soon as it comes out of the oil. Don't cover the fritters to keep them warm or they will go soggy – it's best just to serve them as they are cooked.

Feta and Couscous Fritters

with Schoog

We wanted to try serving our tagine with something other than plain couscous, so we developed these fritters. Deep-fried couscous on its own was no fun, but adding the feta kept the couscous soft and gave the dish a new dimension, the salty feta combining well with the aromatic stew. Then Michael came up with the idea of serving the fritters on their own as a starter with "loads of *schoog*".

SERVES 4-6

a little olive oil
1 Spanish onion, finely chopped
5 garlic cloves, crushed
juice of 2 lemons
pinch of freshly grated nutmeg
250g (9oz) feta cheese
30g (1¼oz) mint leaves, chopped

1 cup of couscous, soaked in boiling
** water to cover, as per packet**
** instructions**
55g (2oz) plain flour
2 eggs, lightly beaten
85g (3oz) dried breadcrumbs
25g (1oz) shelled pistachios, chopped

good handful finely chopped parsley
vegetable oil, for frying
red schoog (page 193), to serve
coriander oil (follow instructions for
** basil oil, page 194), to finish**

1 | Heat the olive oil in a pan. Sauté the onion and garlic until translucent. Put in a blender with the lemon juice, nutmeg and feta, and blend to a thick paste.

2 | Put the paste in a large bowl and fold in the mint and couscous. The mixture should be just firm enough to mould into balls. Roll them into about 12-18 ping-pong-sized balls. Put the flour in a bowl, the beaten eggs in a separate bowl, and mix the breadcrumbs and chopped pistachios together in a third bowl. Roll each ball in flour, then dip in egg, then roll in the breadcrumb-and-pistachio mixture. Repeat the egg and breadcrumb-pistachio coatings again.

3 | Heat 3cm (1¼in) of vegetable oil in a wok or large frying pan until almost smoking and cook the fritters in two to three batches, turning them so they cook evenly, for 3-4 minutes until golden brown. Remove with a slotted spoon and drain on kitchen paper. Put the chopped parsley in a bowl, then roll each fritter in this. Keep warm while you cook the rest in the same way.

4 | Serve three fritters in the middle of each plate, spoon the *schoog* around and trickle with some coriander oil to finish.

Green Banana Fritters

Based on a recipe we picked up in India, here the so-called 'stuffing' is actually mixed through the fritter base rather than sealed inside it. As a result you can make these quite small – from pea-sized up – so they are perfect for nibbles to go with drinks. Many of our customers rave about these fritters, saying they are better than any senna pod or liquorice for restoring regularity...

SERVES 4

3-4 small plantains or green bananas
vegetable oil, for deep-frying
handful of coriander leaves, chopped coconut and coriander chutney (page 204), to serve
chilli coulis (page 182), to serve

STUFFING

1 tbsp each of olive oil and vegetable oil
1 large red chilli, seeded and finely chopped
5cm (2in) fresh root ginger, grated
5-6 shallots or 2 banana shallots, finely chopped

3 garlic cloves
2 tsp sugar
juice of 1 lime
salt

1 | Make the stuffing well ahead. Heat the oils in a large frying pan or wok and cook the chilli for 30 seconds, then stir in the ginger, garlic and shallots, and cook very gently for about 15 minutes. (If the mixture should catch at any point, stir in a few drops of water; don't worry, as a little bit of charring adds to the flavour.) Stir in the sugar until dissolved, then stir in the lime juice and salt to taste. Remove from the heat and leave to sit for 3-4 hours to let the bitterness subside and the flavours develop.

2 | To make the fritters, preheat the oven to 220°C/425°F/gas mark 7 and roast the plantains or green bananas in their skins for 30 minutes, until the skins split and the flesh inside has darkened.

3 | When cool enough to handle, remove the skins and rinse the flesh while still warm as this helps it mash more easily. Peel off the skin and mash the flesh, ideally using a mouli-légumes. If it is a bit too dry to work, put about one-third of it in a food processor and pulse until softer, then mix back in with the rest. Mix the mash well with the cooled 'stuffing' mixture and the coriander, and roll the mixture into 12 ping-pong-sized balls.

4 | To cook the fritters, heat 3cm (1¼in) of vegetable oil in a wok or large frying pan until almost smoking and cook the fritters in two to three batches, turning them so they cook evenly, for 2-3 minutes until golden brown. Remove with a slotted spoon and drain on kitchen paper. Keep warm while you cook the rest in the same way.

5 | To serve, arrange three fritters in the middle of each plate and spoon some chutney and chilli coulis around them.

Roquefort and Fennel Gougères

These arose simply from a wish to produce a savoury profiterole. Roast fennel and blue cheese makes a wonderful flavour combination.

SERVES 4
CHOUX PASTRY
100g (3½oz) butter
125g (4½oz) plain flour
salt and black pepper, to taste
4 eggs

STUFFING
25g (1oz) butter

2 tbsp vegetable oil
**1 medium leek, trimmed and
   finely chopped**
2 garlic cloves, finely chopped
**1 small fennel bulb, cored and
   finely chopped**
good slug of white wine
150g (5½oz) Roquefort cheese

85g (3oz) soft cream cheese

TO SERVE
bunch of rocket leaves
roasted peppers
balsamic reduction (page 198)
toasted walnuts
walnut oil

1 | To make the choux pastry, preheat the oven to 230°C/450°F/gas mark 8. Heat 250ml (9fl oz) water and the butter in a heavy pan, stirring to melt. Bring to the boil, take off the heat and add the flour and a pinch of salt in one go. Stir until thoroughly combined, then return to a moderate heat and continue to stir until the dough forms a coherent mass that comes away from the sides of the pan. Off the heat again, let the dough cool briefly, then add the eggs one by one, stirring in each until it is completely combined.

2 | Line a baking sheet with baking paper and, using an egg cup or the base of a saucer, mark out 12 circles about 2-3cm (about 1in) in diameter. Fill a piping bag with the choux pastry (stand it in a tall narrow jar, pan or vase to make this easier) and pipe spirals to fill each of the circles. Bake for about 20 minutes until dry and lightly golden on the outside, then turn off the heat and leave in the oven for another 10 minutes to dry out completely and to let the outsides get firm. With the handle of a spoon, make holes in the base of each gougère to let the steam escape or else they will go soggy.

3 | To make the stuffing, melt the butter in the oil in a heavy pan over a low heat and sauté the leek and garlic gently until softened. Add the fennel and cook for 3-4 minutes more until that is softened. Add wine to cover and boil rapidly to reduce away most of the liquid. Adjust the seasoning to taste.

4 | Through the hole made in the bases of each *gougère*, scrape out all the soft dough inside. Finish the stuffing by mixing the cheeses into the fennel reduction and use to stuff the *gougères*.

5 | Pile some rocket leaves and snips of roasted red pepper on each plate, arrange three stuffed *gougères* on top of each pile and sprinkle over some balsamic reduction and toasted walnuts. Finish with a drizzle of walnut oil.

Potato Chops

We love these little stuffed potato cakes as they are the sort of thing our parents used to pack as a snack when we went on a trip, so – humble as they are – they still evoke feelings of excitement and mystery in us.

SERVES 4

1kg (2¼lb) floury potatoes
salt and white pepper
plain flour, for dusting
2-3 tbsp vegetable oil
red *schoog* (page 193), to serve

FILLING
2 tbsp vegetable oil
1 heaped tsp panch phoran,

1 chilli, seeded and finely chopped
1 heaped tsp each turmeric, cumin,
 ground coriander and garam masala
large knob of fresh root ginger,
 grated
1 small onion, finely chopped
2 garlic cloves, finely chopped
small handful of corn kernels or
 chopped baby sweetcorn

1 small carrot, diced
1 small courgette, diced
handful of broad beans (about
 5 pods)
handful of coriander leaves, chopped
squeeze of lemon juice

1 | Cook the potatoes in their skins in boiling salted water until tender. Drain and leave to cool. When cool enough to handle, peel off the skins and mash the potatoes with a little salt and white pepper.

2 | For the filling, heat the oil in a wok or large frying pan until quite hot. Add the panch phoran seeds and stir-fry until they pop. Add the chilli and turmeric, stir-fry briefly and turn down the heat slightly. Add the ground coriander, cumin and garam masala, and stir-fry until their aroma rises. Add the ginger, onion and garlic and sweat the mixture gently until the onion is softened. Stir in the corn and carrot and cook for 4-5 minutes. Then add the courgette and broad beans and cook for another 2 minutes. Add the coriander and salt to taste, then turn off the heat and finish with a squeeze of lemon juice.

3 | Pack a deep 6-7cm (2½-2¾in) pastry cutter with mashed potato until slightly less than half full. With the back of a spoon, make a recess in the middle of the potato layer. Pile the filling into the centre of that recess and then top with another layer of potato and pack down well again. Gently shake or ease the potato cake out of the pastry cutter (you may need to go round the edge with a knife) and make three more in the same way. Chill for about 30 minutes.

4 | Dust the potato cakes in flour, shaking off any excess, and fry in hot oil for about 3 minutes on each side until nicely browned. Drain briefly on kitchen paper and serve the potato cakes with the *schoog* dotted around them.

Thelma Pancakes

The grandmother of Adrian's closest childhood friend, Michael Gazal, was known to us as Aunty Thelma, and this is how she made pancakes every Friday, hence the name in tribute. Every time Adrian makes pancakes it reminds him of the summer of '76, when he played football with the Moses brothers every day. Mama Moses made lots of food for them all and stuffed their fridge and freezer, but the eldest brother, Moses Moses, decided it was going to be "the year of the pancake" and they would go back to their place after the game and make pancakes. Eventually Mama Moses realized that her piles of food weren't going down and caught them making pancakes. She was affronted: 'I make them all lovely food and they ignore it... if I were to make them pancakes they would complain!'

Seitan is a form of inexpensive meat-free protein made from wheat flour that was originally developed by Buddhist monks in China, but was embraced in a big way by the macrobiotic movement in the 1960s. Looking a bit like soggy wholemeal bread, but with a sharp nutty taste, it beats tofu hollow in being good at absorbing flavours in cooking. Here we cut it into strips and fry it with ginger, coriander and spring onions. Do this and add some soy sauce, and you can serve it like mock duck with steamed pancakes and plum sauce, with a julienne of spring onions and cucumber.

These stuffed pancakes also make really nice canapés if sliced into thick discs. If you are going to make them with this in mind, it is a good idea to brush the rolled pancakes with beaten egg before frying them as this will help them hold together when sliced. Serve with mango chutney (page 205) or harissa (page 197).

SERVES 4

SEITAN
1kg (2¼lb) plain flour, plus more for dusting
about 500ml (18fl oz) cold water
2 tbsp vegetable oil
splash of olive oil
2 tbsp chopped spring onion greens
black pepper, to taste
handful of coriander leaves, chopped

SOAKING STOCK
large chunk of fresh root ginger
1 lemongrass stalk
2 tbsp soy sauce

PANCAKES
1 large egg
200g (7oz) plain flour
large pinch of salt
about 300ml (10fl oz) milk
large pinch coriander leaves, chopped
vegetable oil and butter, for frying

FILLING
1 tsp toasted black sesame seeds
2 tbsp olive oil
2 shallots, finely chopped
1 tbsp each of cumin and ground coriander
2 garlic cloves, finely chopped
small knob of fresh root ginger

75g (2¾oz) shelled peas or broad beans
55g (2oz) corn kernels or chopped baby sweetcorn
pinch of coriander leaves, chopped

SALAD
large bunch of rocket
good handful of each of mint and coriander leaves
2 tbsp olive oil
juice of ½ lime

TO SERVE
red schoog (page 193)

1 | Well ahead, start the seitan. Sift the flour into a bowl and add just enough water to make a loose but manageable dough. Knead for 20 minutes on a well-floured surface until spongy and, when pressed, it bounces back. Put in a container, cover with cold water, put a lid on and refrigerate for at least 5-6 hours, preferably overnight.

2 | Put the soaked dough in a colander. Rinse it under cold running water, kneading it to wash out the starch, until it becomes stringy and the water runs clear. You may have to change to warm water sometimes to keep it soft.

3 | Make the soaking stock by adding the ingredients to just enough simmering water to cover the seitan, and cooking for 5 minutes. Add the seitan and poach it for 20 minutes, covered, until doubled in size. Leave to cool in the stock.

4 | For the pancake batter, crack the egg into a bowl, sift in the flour and salt to make a thick mass, then add just enough milk to give a creamy consistency that coats the back of a spoon. Stir in the coriander and leave to rest for 30 minutes.

5 | Drain the seitan. Cut into slices, then cut those into bite-sized pieces. Heat the oils in a wok or frying pan and stir-fry the seitan with the spring onion for 3-4 minutes until crisp. Add the pepper and coriander, stir-fry for a few seconds more and put in a bowl.

6 | For the filling, wipe the pan with paper towels and toast the sesame seeds in it. Add the oil and sweat the shallots, spices, garlic and ginger over a low heat for 5-6 minutes (add a little water if it sticks). Add the vegetables and 75g (2¾oz) seitan and cook for 2-3 minutes, then add the coriander. Leave to cool.

7 | For the pancakes, heat a little oil in a 20cm (8in) pan. Add just enough mixture to coat the pan, tilting, and cook for 2-3 minutes until bubbles appear. Flip and cook the other side for the same time. Cook three more pancakes, wiping out the pan with a paper towel and adding a little more oil between each. Allow the pancakes to cool.

8 | When cool, put one-quarter of the filling in the middle of a pancake, roll up and fold in – left and right sides in, then near side up and over – and continue to roll, tucking in the sides. Repeat with the other pancakes. Fry the pancakes in hot oil and butter for 2-3 minutes on each side. Drain on kitchen paper.

9 | Toss the salad leaves in the oil and lime juice. Pile on each plate. Halve each pancake across at an angle and sit, cut sides uppermost, on the salad. Add dots of *schoog*.

Risotto Cakes

This variation on the risotto formula – very much in the Italian tradition – makes an unusual starter or snack.

SERVES 4

350g (12oz) peeled and seeded squash, cut into 1cm (½in) dice
salt and black pepper
2 tbsp vegetable oil, plus a little more for coating
2 large pinches thyme leaves, chopped
85g (3oz) butter

2-3 banana shallots or 4-5 small ones, finely chopped
pinch of rosemary leaves, chopped
200g (7oz) risotto rice
dash of white wine
2 garlic cloves, finely chopped
about 350ml (12fl oz) vegetable stock (page 40), simmering

55g (2oz) Parmesan, freshly grated
juice of ½ lemon
200g (7oz) Taleggio cheese, cubed
drizzle of truffle oil, plus more to finish (optional)
12 asparagus spears

1 | Preheat the oven to 180°C/350°F/gas mark 4 and line a roasting tray with foil or baking paper. Season the squash and toss in a little oil with half the thyme. Arrange in a single layer on the roasting tray and roast for 10-12 minutes until tender.

2 | Heat the 2 tbsp of oil and one-third of the butter in a deep heavy-based pan. Add the shallots and rosemary and sauté until the shallots are softened. Add the rice with the remaining thyme and stir until well coated in the fat. Increase the heat, add the wine and simmer gently. When most of the wine has been absorbed, stir in a large ladleful of the hot stock. Cook over a moderate heat, stirring every few minutes and adding more stock as it is absorbed. Continue cooking and adding stock (or boiling water if that runs out) until the grains of rice taste creamy but still have a nut of hardness in their centres. You are probably talking about only 15 minutes cooking, as opposed to the 15-25 needed to finish risotto in the usual away. Also aim for a drier consistency than ordinary risotto.

3 | Take off the heat and stir in the Parmesan and remaining butter, with seasoning to taste if necessary and lemon juice to taste. Leave to cool, stirring from time to time.

4 | When cool, mix the rice with the squash, Taleggio and truffle oil, and form into 12 patties (you can pack the mixture into an oiled pastry ring if you like). Chill for about 20 minutes.

5 | In a little more vegetable oil in a frying pan, or on a lightly oiled griddle over a fairly high heat, sear the cakes until nicely coloured on both sides.

6 | At the same time, coat the asparagus spears lightly with oil and sear in the same way until just tender.

7 | Arrange three risotto cakes on each plate and then arrange the asparagus spears on top of them. If you like, finish with a few more drops of truffle oil.

Gate Gnocchi

Outside of Italy we have usually found gnocchi unbearably heavy and rubbery, and this has made us determined to find a way of making them with as little flour as necessary so that they are light and let the full flavour of the potato come through. We serve our gnocchi with a wide range of accompaniments, depending on the season and what's available – here with wilted spinach and sautéed wood blewit mushrooms.

SERVES 4
125g (4½oz) peeled and seeded
  butternut squash or pumpkin
a little vegetable oil
250g (9oz) dry mashed potato
1 egg yolk
55g (2oz) plain flour
1 tbsp freshly grated Parmesan
salt

SAUCE
200g (7oz) leeks, trimmed, well
  rinsed and finely chopped
knob of butter
½ tbsp thyme leaves, chopped
splash of dry white wine
400ml (14fl oz) double cream
55g (2oz) mascarpone cheese

TO SERVE
8 wood blewits or oyster or
  field mushrooms
2 tbsp olive oil
a little butter
150g (5½oz) small leaf spinach
parsley sprigs, to garnish (optional)

1 | Preheat the oven to 200°C/400°F/gas mark 6. Cut up the squash or pumpkin. Brush with oil, lay cut side down in a roasting tin and place in the oven for 30-40 minutes, or until soft. Transfer to a food processor and purée until smooth.

2 | Bring a large pan of water to the boil. Mix the purée with the dry mashed potato, egg yolk, flour and Parmesan. Roll into a long sausage shape, then cut at an angle into pieces about 2cm (¾in) thick. (If you like, you can mould them into rugby ball shapes as shown, for a more elegant presentation.) Salt the boiling water and poach these gnocchi in it until they rise to the surface. Drain well.

3 | Slice the mushrooms if large and sauté them in the olive oil until coloured and softened.

4 | While the mushrooms are sautéing, make the sauce. Sauté the leeks in the butter with the thyme for 5 minutes until soft but not coloured. Add the wine, cream and mascarpone and bring to the boil. Push through a sieve and set aside.

5 | In a heavy pan over a fairly high heat, melt the butter and then wilt the spinach leaves briefly in it.

6 | Pile the wilted spinach in the centre of four warmed plates, then arrange the gnocchi on top of that and pour over the sauce. Garnish with the mushrooms, and a parsley sprig if you like, and serve.

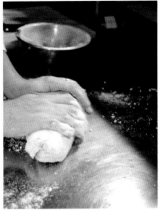

1 | 2
3 | 4
    5

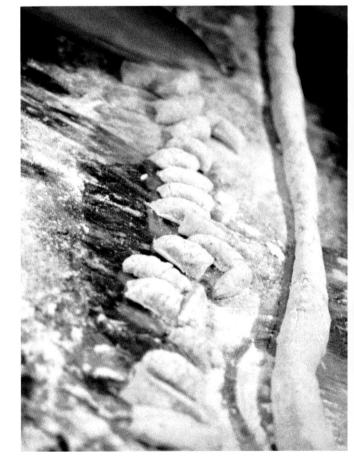

Gnocchi

We know gnocchi are just another form of dumpling, but we love dumplings of all sorts and these gnocchi are a delicious cross between dumplings and pasta. They are also dead easy to make, which is why they are probably the form of pasta most commonly made by Italians.

One of the real virtues for us of these little Italian nuggets is that they can be made from a wide range of bases apart from wheat – for example potato flour or mashed potato, polenta (cornmeal) and even pumpkin, as in the *gnocchi di zucca* of Mantua – giving you the opportunity of making the dumpling using vegetables only (although a little ordinary flour is usually added to help the mixture cohere).

Dressings for gnocchi can be as simple as melted butter, some grated cheese or a spoonful or two of pesto (any one of our pestos on pages 178-181 will work well). Various herbs, including sage, basil and rosemary, are often sprinkled over gnocchi, as are, more unusually, ground cinnamon and crumbled amaretti biscuits.

To make the gnocchi:

1 | Mix the base ingredients together well to form a malleable dough. The secret of making gnocchi is getting the dough as light as possible without it being liable to disintegrate during cooking. If you've used a floury variety of potato, it is advisable to add a beaten egg yolk to the mixture (see the recipe on page 76) but if you use a waxy potato you may not need the egg. Bring a large pan of water to the boil.

2&3 | Roll the gnocchi mixture into a long sausage shape.

4&5 | Cut at an angle into pieces about 2cm (¾in) thick. If you like, you can mould them into rugby-ball shapes as shown, for more elegant presentation; the Italians often mark them all over with the prongs of a fork, as this helps them cling on to any sauce or dressing when they are served.

Salt the boiling water and poach the gnocchi in it until they rise to the surface. Remove with a slotted spoon and drain on a clean tea-towel.

Involtini

The idea of this dish was to use the unbeatable flavours of the classic *insalata tricolore* in a new way. Aubergine was the obvious vegetable to wrap the other ingredients in.

SERVES 4

2 large aubergines
2 tbsp olive oil
4 tbsp basil pesto (page 178)
3-4 large plum tomatoes, skinned
  and cut into 16 large slices
salt
200g (7oz) *mozzarella di bufala*,
  cut into 8 slices
75g (2¾oz) Parmesan, freshly grated
seasoned plain flour, for coating

1 egg, beaten
55g (2oz) soft breadcrumbs
handful of chopped parsley
sun-dried tomato and lentil salsa
  (page 187), to serve

TOMATO AND LENTIL SAUCE
150g (5½oz) Puy lentils
2 tbsp olive oil
1 onion, finely chopped

red chilli, seeded and finely chopped
large sprig of thyme
1 small red pepper, seeded
1 small carrot, finely chopped
1 x 400g can chopped tomatoes
1 tbsp sun-dried tomato pesto
  (page 180) or purée
splash each of red wine and
  balsamic vinegar
½ tbsp sugar

1 | For the sauce, soak the lentils in cold water for 30 minutes.

2 | Preheat a dry griddle until good and hot. Trimming off the sides of the aubergines, cut each lengthwise into four nice big slices. Brush these on both sides with oil and griddle over a high heat until softened and nicely seared on both sides. Set aside to cool.

3 | While the aubergines are cooling, make the tomato and lentil sauce. Drain the lentils. Heat the olive oil in a saucepan. Cook the onion, chilli and thyme briefly in the hot oil. Finely chop the red pepper, then add it with the chopped carrot and cook briefly. Stir in the remaining ingredients, including the drained lentils, bring to a simmer and cook gently for about 30 minutes, until you have a nice thick sauce.

4 | Spread the grilled aubergine slices thickly with the pesto. Sprinkle salt over the tomato slices, then arrange two slices of tomato and one of mozzarella just in from one end of each slice of aubergine. Sprinkle the Parmesan over that. Roll up the slices to make compact packages. Dip each in seasoned flour, then in egg and finally in the breadcrumbs mixed with the parsley, shaking off excess in each case. Chill for about 30 minutes.

5 | Preheat the oven to 180°C/350°F/gas mark 4. Bake the *involtini* for about 10 minutes until the coating is nicely crisp and lightly coloured.

6 | Serve two *involtini* on each plate, sitting on mounds of the lentil sauce.

Paneer Kibbeh
with Stuffed Paratha and Green Mango Chutney

This makes a perfect summer lunch. Use haloumi if you can't find paneer. Cut the cheese into fat cubes if you are using skewers for the barbecue.

SERVES 4

200g (7oz) paneer (Indian cheese),
  cut into 12 cubes or flat strips
1 red onion, halved and sliced
cherry tomatoes (optional
  if barbecuing)
chunks of red and yellow pepper
  (optional if barbecuing)
green mango chutney (page 205)
lemon wedges and parsley sprigs

MARINADE

4-5 tbsp mustard oil, plus more
  for brushing
2 red chillies

1 red pepper
1 tbsp cumin seeds
½ cinnamon stick, in pieces
1 star anise
seeds of 3 black and 3 green
  cardamom pods
1 tbsp black mustard seeds
3-4 shallots, finely chopped
4-5 garlic cloves, finely chopped
chunk of fresh root ginger, chopped
1 tbsp smoked paprika
handful each of mint and coriander
  leaves, coarsely chopped
100g (3½oz) plain yoghurt

STUFFED PARATHA

125g (4½oz) chapati flour
125g (4½oz) plain flour
1 tbsp mustard oil
1 tsp salt
1 largish potato, cooked and
  mashed dry
small handful of coriander leaves,
  chopped
1 tbsp ground coriander
juice of ½ lemon
vegetable oil, for brushing
melted butter, for brushing

1 | Well ahead, make the marinade. Lightly brush the chillies and pepper with a little of the mustard oil and roast. Meanwhile, in a dry, heavy frying pan, gently toast the cumin seeds, cinnamon, star anise, cardamom and mustard seeds until they give off their aromas, then grind them together using a pestle and mortar.

2 | Sweat the chilli, shallots, garlic and ginger in a little of the mustard oil until softened. Stir in the smoked paprika followed by the herbs and take off the heat.

3 | Stir into the yoghurt with the spice mix and remaining mustard oil. Purée the roasted chillies and pepper in a food processor and mix into the marinade. Stir the paneer into the marinade and leave for at least 3 hours or, better still, overnight (in the fridge), stirring from time to time if you like.

4 | To make the *paratha*, in a bowl mix the flours, mustard oil and salt with just enough warm water to give a workable dough. Knead for 3-4 minutes, then gather into a ball, oil lightly and leave to rest in warm place in the bowl, covered with a clean cloth, for 30-40 minutes.

5 | To make the stuffing, mix the mashed potato, coriander leaves, ground seeds and the lemon juice together with salt to taste.

6 | Cut the rested dough into largish billiard-ball shapes and roll each to a round about 2mm (⅟₁₆in) thick. Put about 1½ tsp of the stuffing mix in the centre and fold the edges up around the stuffing to seal it in. Roll again to a flat round.

7 | When ready to cook, brush both sides of each *paratha* with a mix of vegetable oil and melted butter and cook them by pressing them down in a very hot frying pan for 2-3 minutes on each side, until nicely browned. Set aside in a warm place.

8 | Cook the marinated paneer (taking a good coating of marinade with each piece) on a very hot griddle pan or in a very hot dry frying pan for 2-3 minutes on each side until nicely coloured all over. Cook the red onion with them. Alternatively if barbecuing, thread cubes of the cheese on metal skewers interspersed with cherry tomatoes and pepper chunks.

9 | Serve the paneer with the onion, *parathas* and green mango chutney. Garnish with lemon wedges and parsley leaves if you like.

Grilled Haloumi
with Chickpeas

People just love grilled haloumi, and its texture goes so well with that of the chickpea salsa. Cut the cheese into fat cubes if you are going to thread them on to skewers for the barbecue; flat strips let the marinade into the cheese more readily.

SERVES 4
350g (12oz) haloumi cheese
harissa (page 197), to serve
large slices of skinned roasted red
** pepper, to serve (optional)**

CHICKPEA SALSA
125g (4½oz) cooked chickpeas
handful each of coriander and mint
** leaves, chopped**
3-4 tbsp olive oil
juice of 1 lemon
4-5 spring onions, chopped

1 | First make the salsa by mixing all the ingredients together.

2 | Cut the haloumi into 1cm (½in) slices or 8mm (⅜in) cubes and leave to drain on kitchen paper so it will crisp up better during cooking.

3 | Preheat a griddle or dry, heavy frying pan until very hot and then sear the haloumi slices or cubes until well browned, turning once.

4 | Pile the salsa in the middle of four serving plates and arrange the haloumi on top. Spoon some harissa around the outside and garnish with the red pepper strips, if using them.

Chanterelle Mousse

When making a mushroom *duxelles* for this sort of dish, or even as a stuffing, we aim to have a ratio by weight of mushroom to shallot of three to one. In the restaurant, in season, we serve this mousse with the wild mushroom "cauliflower fungus", which we lightly sauté and then sit on top of the turned-out round of mousse.

SERVES 4

large knob of butter
about 350g (12oz) shallots,
  preferably banana shallots,
  finely chopped
large pinch each of thyme and
  rosemary leaves, finely chopped
salt and black pepper

1kg (2½lb) chanterelles, torn into
  strips
a good splash of white wine
500g (18oz) ricotta cheese
2 tbsp freshly grated Parmesan
bruschetta, to serve
chopped chives, to garnish (optional)

1 | Melt the butter in a frying pan and sauté the shallots with the herbs and seasoning to taste briefly until softening, then add the mushrooms and cook, stirring frequently, for 5-6 minutes until softened. Add the white wine and cook rapidly until almost all the liquid has gone. Leave to cool.

2 | When cool, purée the contents of the pan with the two cheeses in a blender, turn out into a bowl, and chill for at least 40 minutes, until firm.

3 | Spoon the chilled mousse into quenelles (mould with 2 dsp), arrange on serving plates and serve with bruschetta. Alternatively, you can pile the mousse into ramekins and garnish with chopped chives. In the restaurant, we line the ramekins with clingfilm and turn out as a neat round.

Parmesan Tartlets

with Roasted Tomatoes, Pesto and Asparagus

This was devised to give us a tart for summer, without a heavy cream and egg filling and full of nice simple flavours – as well as the red and green colours of the season.

SERVES 4
basil pesto (page 178)
1 *mozzarella di bufala*, **sliced**
wild rocket, to serve
handful of chervil sprigs, to serve
basil oil (page 194) and balsamic
  reduction (page 198), to garnish

ROAST TOMATOES
6 ripe plum tomatoes, blanched
  and skinned

olive oil, for brushing
salt
1 garlic clove, thinly sliced

SHORTCRUST PASTRY
400g (14oz) plain flour
salt and black pepper
150g (5½oz) butter
75g (2¾oz) Parmesan, grated

ASPARAGUS
24 slender asparagus stalks,
  preferably wild
5 tbsp extra virgin olive oil
1 tbsp lemon juice

1 | Well ahead, ideally the day before, prepare the roast tomatoes. Preheat the oven to 140°C/275°F/gas mark 1. Halve the tomatoes and arrange on a wire rack. Brush well with olive oil, season with salt and drop a slice of garlic on top of each tomato half. Put in the oven and cook for 3 hours, or simply switch off the oven and leave the tomatoes in it overnight.

2 | At least an hour before you want to serve, make the pastry. In a food processor, pulse the flour, a pinch of salt and the butter together until the mixture resembles breadcrumbs. Add the cheese and pepper to taste, and pulse again briefly to mix. Then, bit by bit, add just enough cold water to bring it to a smooth malleable dough. Roll it into a ball, cover with clingfilm and chill for 30 minutes.

3 | Preheat the oven to 190°C/375°F/gas mark 5. Roll the chilled pastry out to a large rectangle and use to line four 5cm (2in) tartlet tins. Don't trim the edges, but fold them over so they can be trimmed after initial baking. Prick the bases lightly with a fork. Line the pastry cases with baking paper, weight with baking beans and bake blind for 15 minutes. Remove the beans and lining paper and trim the pastry edges. (Leave the oven on.)

4 | Put three tomato halves in each tartlet, spread with basil pesto and top with slices of mozzarella. Bake for 10 minutes.

5 | While the tartlets are baking, prepare the asparagus. Blanch the stalks by dipping them in and out of a large pan of boiling water, then refresh in cold water. Drain and pat dry. Make a dressing by mixing the olive oil with the lemon juice and seasoning to taste. Use to dress the asparagus stalks.

6 | Serve the tartlets warm or cold, each one topped with two asparagus stalks and perhaps a sprig of basil, set on a bed of wild rocket mixed with chervil leaves, some basil oil and some balsamic reduction.

Three-onion Tart

The sweetness of the caramelized red onions works well with the leek and onion custard and the nuttiness of the pastry.

SERVES 10-12

30g (1¼oz) butter
2 red onions, halved and sliced into half moons
1 tbsp muscovado sugar
splash of balsamic vinegar
2 garlic cloves, finely chopped
2 small leeks, halved lengthwise and then sliced across into half moons

2 banana shallots or 3-4 ordinary shallots, halved and sliced into half moons
good slosh of white wine
4 eggs
250ml (9fl oz) double cream
500ml (18fl oz) crème fraîche

PECAN PASTRY
225g (8oz) plain flour, plus more for dusting
115g (4oz) chilled butter
good handful of shelled pecan nuts, finely chopped
salt and black pepper, to taste

1 | For the pastry, sift the flour into a bowl, grate in the butter then rub it in with the fingers until it resembles fine breadcrumbs. Add the pecans and salt and pepper and then, using a round-bladed knife, cut in enough cold water for it to bind into balls of dough. Gather these into one ball and leave to rest for 20 minutes.

2 | On a well-floured surface, roll the dough out into a round large enough to line a 28cm (11in) tart pan, regularly turning the dough by 90 degrees to keep it circular. Leave to rest for 20 minutes.

3 | Preheat the oven to 200°C/400°F/gas mark 6. Line the tart pan with the pastry, pressing it into the tin and spreading it from the base into the corners. Leave the excess overhanging and press it in so it is tight against the tin. Chill for 10-20 minutes.

4 | Line the pastry case with baking paper, weight with baking beans and bake blind for 15-20 minutes, until uniformly light golden and cooked, with no patches of moist uncooked pastry. Remove the beans and paper after 10 minutes to help it dry out.

5 | While the pastry case is cooking, in a frying pan heat half the butter and very gently sweat the red onions in it with the sugar and balsamic vinegar for about 15 minutes, stirring from time to time, until nicely caramelized.

6 | In a separate large frying pan, melt the remaining butter over a gentle heat, add the garlic and cook briefly, then stir in the leeks and shallots and sweat gently for 5-6 minutes, until just softening. Add the white wine and cook over a high heat, stirring all the time, until almost all the liquid has gone.

7 | In a large bowl, beat the eggs, stir in the cream and crème fraîche, and season generously to taste.

8 | Take the pastry case from the oven and turn the oven down to 180°C/350°F/gas mark 4. Remove the beans or rice and the lining paper from the pastry case. Trim off the excess pastry at the edges. Arrange the leeks and shallots in the bottom of the pastry case. Pour the egg-and-cream mixture evenly over the contents of the tart and tap the baking sheet on a hard surface to make sure it gets into every nook and cranny.

9 | Put in the cooler oven and cook for 40-45 minutes, until just nicely set (when you shake the tart gently it no longer wobbles). Scatter the red onion over the top while still warm. Serve warm or cold.

Butternut and Gruyère Tart

This is our vegetarian version of that old standby, quiche lorraine.

SERVES 10-12
large knob of butter
2 banana shallots or 3-4 ordinary shallots, sliced into half moons
350g (12oz) peeled and seeded butternut squash, thinly sliced into half-moon shapes
handful of basil leaves
225g (8oz) Gruyère cheese, grated or broken into lumps
4 eggs
250ml (9fl oz) double cream
500ml (18fl oz) crème fraîche

THYME PASTRY
225g (8oz) plain flour, plus more for dusting
115g (4oz) chilled butter
leaves of few sprigs of thyme, chopped
salt and black pepper

1 | First make the pastry. Sift the flour into a bowl, grate in the butter, then rub it in with the fingers until it resembles fine breadcrumbs. Add the thyme, salt and pepper to taste and then, using a round-bladed knife, cut in just enough cold water for it to bind into balls of dough. Gather these together into one ball and leave to rest for 20 minutes.

2 | On a well-floured surface, roll the dough out into a round large enough to line a 28cm (11in) tart pan, regularly turning the dough by 90 degrees to keep the shape circular. Leave to rest for another 20 minutes.

3 | Preheat the oven to 200°C/400°F/gas mark 6. Line the tart pan with the pastry, pressing it into the tin and spreading it from the base into the corners to prevent shrinking. Leave the excess overhanging and press it in so that it is tight against the tin. Chill for another 10-20 minutes.

4 | Line the pastry case with baking paper, weight with baking beans (or rice) and bake blind for 15-20 minutes until uniformly light golden and cooked through, with no patches of moist uncooked pastry (as the pastry won't cook much more once filled). Remove the beans and paper after 10 minutes to help it dry out.

5 | While the pastry case is cooking, in a frying pan, heat the butter and sauté the shallots gently until just softened.

6 | Blanch the squash in boiling salted water for 1-2 minutes, until just becoming tender. Refresh in cold water, drain well and pat dry.

7 | Take the pastry case from the oven and turn the oven down to 180°C/350°F/gas mark 4. Remove the beans or rice and the lining paper from the pastry case. Scatter the cooked shallots over the bottom of the pastry case. Arrange a layer of half the squash over the shallots decoratively in concentric circles and sprinkle over the basil leaves, followed by half the cheese. Follow with another layer of squash and finally a layer of cheese.

8 | In a large bowl, beat the eggs, stir in the cream and crème fraîche, and season generously. Pour evenly over the tart and tap the baking sheet on a hard surface to make sure it gets all the way down.

9 | Bake for 40-45 minutes until just nicely set (when you shake the tart gently it no longer wobbles). Serve warm or cold.

Trompette and Leek Tart

This is yet another dish we put together for our fungi or mushroom fest. We wanted to ensure our menus remained balanced – with lots of mushroom flavour but without the feeling of too much mushroom.

SERVES 10-12

30g (1¼oz) butter
55g (2oz) trompettes-des-morts mushrooms
sprinkling of chopped thyme
salt and black pepper
2 garlic cloves, finely chopped
2 small leeks, halved lengthwise and then sliced across into half moons

2 banana shallots or 3-4 ordinary shallots, halved and sliced into half moons
good slosh of white wine
4 eggs
250ml (9fl oz) double cream
500ml (18oz) crème fraîche

THYME PASTRY
225g (8oz) plain flour, plus more for dusting
115g (4oz) chilled butter
few sprigs of thyme, leaves stripped and finely chopped
salt and black pepper, to taste

1 | For the pastry, sift the flour into a bowl, grate in the butter, then rub it in until it resembles fine breadcrumbs. Add the thyme, salt and pepper then, using a round-bladed knife, cut in enough cold water for it to bind into balls. Gather these into one ball and leave to rest for 20 minutes.

2 | On a well-floured surface, roll the dough out into a round large enough to line a 28cm (11in) tart pan, regularly turning the dough by 90 degrees to keep it circular. Leave to rest for 20 minutes.

3 | Preheat the oven to 200°C/400°F/gas mark 6. Line the tart pan with the pastry, pressing it into the tin and spreading it from the base into the corners. Leave the excess overhanging and press it in so it is tight against the tin. Chill for 10-20 minutes.

4 | Line the pastry case with baking paper, weight with baking beans (or rice) and bake blind for 15-20 minutes, until uniformly light golden and cooked, with no patches of moist uncooked pastry. Remove the beans and paper after 10 minutes to help it dry out.

5 | While the pastry case is cooking, in a frying pan heat half the butter and gently sweat the mushrooms with the herbs and seasoning in half the butter for a minute, stirring, until wilted.

6 | In a large frying pan, melt the remaining butter over a gentle heat, add the garlic and cook briefly, then stir in the leeks and shallots and sweat gently for 5-6 minutes, until softening. Add the white wine and cook over a high heat, stirring all the time, until almost all the liquid has gone.

7 | In a large bowl, beat the eggs, stir in the cream and crème fraîche, and season generously.

8 | Take the pastry case from the oven and turn the oven down to 180°C/350°F/gas mark 4. Remove the beans or rice and the lining paper from the pastry case. Trim off the excess pastry at the edges. Arrange the leeks and shallots in the bottom of the pastry case. Pour the egg-and-cream mixture evenly over the contents of the tart and tap the baking sheet on a hard surface to make sure it gets into every nook and cranny.

9 | Put in the oven and cook for 30 minutes until just beginning to set. Scatter the mushrooms over the top and return to the oven for 10-15 minutes until set (when you shake the tart gently it no longer wobbles). Serve warm or cold.

Tempura Mushrooms

People love this treatment of mushrooms, as it brings out their full flavour and the crunchy coating emphasizes their texture. It is an excellent way of appreciating the full whack of the taste of a mushroom and the subtle differences in the flavours of varieties. You need to choose good-sized, well-shaped mushrooms, as most of them remain whole.

SERVES 4
oil, for deep-frying
8 oyster mushrooms
4 or 8 shiitake mushrooms
4 ceps, cut into 2mm (⅟₁₆in)
 thick slices
4 chanterelles
sweet chilli sauce, to serve

TEMPURA BATTER
1 egg
about 80ml (2½fl oz) cold beer
1 cup cornflour
1 tbsp black sesame seeds
1 tbsp white sesame seeds

1 | To make the tempura batter, beat the egg in a medium bowl, then mix in most of the beer, reserving a few spoonfuls. Tip in the flour and sesame seeds and mix quickly (don't overmix or you will get a tough batter – a few lumps is a good sign). If the batter seems too thick, add some or all of the remaining beer.

2 | In a wok, heat the oil for deep-frying until very hot. Dip the mushrooms in the batter quickly, allowing excess batter to drip off, and fry in batches of two to three at a time until nicely golden brown – about 2-3 minutes. Drain briefly on kitchen paper.

 3 | Serve the mushrooms as quickly as possible, in a circle on each plate, with a ring of the sweet chilli sauce around them.

Stuffed Ceps

The idea of this dish is to make the ceps, when presented on the plate, look as if nothing has been done to them. The diner then finds the delicious surprise stuffing inside.

SERVES 4

4 medium cep mushrooms
a little butter
3 shallots, finely chopped
few sprigs of oregano, plus more
 for garnish
150g (5½oz) ricotta cheese

25g (1oz) Parmesan, freshly grated
handful of soft breadcrumbs
a little vegetable oil
truffle oil, to serve
1 large plum tomato, for garnish
 (optional)

1 | Preheat the oven to 200°C/400°F/gas mark 6. Take the caps off the stalks and hollow out the stalks. Chop the inner parts of the stalks.

2 | Heat a little butter, then fry the shallots and oregano until softened. Add the chopped mushroom stalks and cook until softened. In a bowl, mix this with the ricotta and Parmesan, then bind with the breadcrumbs.

3 | Using a teaspoon or piping bag, stuff the mushroom stalks with the mixture. Set the caps back in place on top of the stalks (the filling should help hold them in place). Arrange the reassembled mushrooms on a baking sheet.

4 | Brush the stalks and caps with a little oil and bake in the preheated oven for 10 minutes.

5 | Serve with a ring of truffle oil around each seemingly undisturbed cep and garnish with some more oregano sprigs. If you want a dash of colour on the plate, make a tomato concassé by quartering the tomato, scooping out the insides, patting the flesh dry with kitchen paper, then dicing.

Carciofi e Porcini
(Artichokes and Ceps)

Artichokes make tasty receptacles for stuffings. This dish is our take on the classic Roman *carciofi alla giudia*, or Jewish artichokes, that is usually made using young artichokes that have barely developed a choke, so the whole thing can be eaten. According to Claudia Roden in *The Book of Jewish Food*, deep-frying was a speciality of the Jewish ghetto in Rome.

SERVES 4
8 baby globe artichokes
salt
lemon juice
vegetable oil, for shallow- or deep-frying
aïoli (page 190), to serve

MUSHROOM DUXELLES
2 tbsp olive oil
25g (1oz) butter

1 large onion, finely chopped
2-3 garlic cloves, finely chopped
sprig of thyme, finely chopped
sprig of rosemary, tarragon or basil, finely chopped
dash of white wine
500g (18oz) ceps, portobello or chestnut mushrooms, finely chopped

3-4 rehydrated dried porcini or a cep stock cube made up with a little boiling water or a few drops of truffle oil (for cultivated mushrooms)

TEMPURA BATTER
1 egg
about 80ml (2½fl oz) cold beer
1 cup cornflour

1 | Slice off the top third of each artichoke and peel away most of each stalk to remove the dark green. Peel off two or three of the layers of outer leaves and, using a teaspoon or melon baller, scoop out and discard the hairy choke in the centre.

2 | Bring a large pan of salted water, acidulated with lemon juice, to the boil and drop in the prepared artichokes. Cover with a plate to keep them totally submerged and simmer for 6-7 minutes, until tender (test with the tip of a sharp knife at the point where the stalk joins the cup). Drain upside down to let all the water escape.

3 | To make the mushroom *duxelles*, heat the oil and butter in a large heavy pan and sweat the onion, garlic and herbs until softened. Add the white wine and cook until almost all of it has gone. Add the chopped mushrooms with seasoning to taste and continue to sweat for 2-3 minutes until softened. If necessary – i.e., if you are using the cultivated portobello or chestnut mushrooms – add the chopped rehydrated porcini, made-up stock cube or truffle oil.

4 | When the artichokes are cool enough to handle, squeeze them gently around the edges to get rid of any moisture still lingering between the leaves. Pat dry inside and out. Stuff the cavities of the artichokes with the duxelles.

5 | Make the *tempura* batter. Beat the egg in a medium bowl, mix in most of the beer, reserving a few spoonfuls. Tip in the flour and mix quickly (don't overmix or you will get a tough batter – a few lumps is a good sign). If the batter seems too thick, add some or all of the remaining beer.

6 | Heat the oil for shallow- or deep-frying. Dip the artichokes one by one in the batter, letting excess drip off, and fry for 2-3 minutes, turning, until nicely coloured (you may have to do this in batches).

7 | Serve two artichokes on each plate with a big blob of *aïoli*.

Three Artichokes Salad

We created this dish mostly because we really want to bring all three types of artichoke to people's attention.

SERVES 4

150g (5½oz) Jerusalem artichokes
sprinkling each of thyme and
** rosemary leaves, chopped**
salt and black pepper
100g (3½oz) *crosnes* (Chinese
** artichokes)**
6 baby globe artichokes or 2 large
** globe artichokes**

1 lemon, juiced
a little extra virgin olive oil
good handful each of rocket and
** baby spinach leaves**
few drops of truffle oil

1 | Preheat the oven to 180°/350°F/gas mark 4. Peel the Jerusalem artichokes and slice them thinly. Scatter in a foil-lined baking tray with the herbs and some seasoning, and roast for 10 minutes. Roast the *crosnes* whole for 5 minutes on a separate tray in the oven, adding seasoning only. Allow both to cool.

2 | At the same time, prepare the globe artichokes and poach them in salted water, acidulated with lemon juice. Refresh in cold water, pat dry and drizzle with a little olive oil. Cut each into eight wedges.

3 | To serve, toss the rocket and spinach with the truffle oil, salt and pepper, and a squeeze of lemon juice. Arrange on four plates and scatter each with equal amounts of each artichoke.

Artichokes

(Cynara Cardunculus Scolymus; Helianthus Tuberosus; Stachys Sieboldii)

We use all three types of artichoke in the restaurant, sometimes all three together as in our Three Artichokes Salad (page 100). The globe artichoke (*cynara cardunculus scolymus*), Jerusalem artichoke (*helianthus tuberosus*) and Chinese artichoke or crosne (*stachys sieboldii*) are, in fact, perhaps only really related in flavour.

The globe artichoke is a Mediterranean variety of thistle in the sunflower family and it is actually the flower head that we eat. The Jerusalem artichoke, the tuber of a perennial sunflower, originated in America (where it is now often referred to as the sunchoke) and was first brought to Europe in the early 17th century and imported to Britain via Italy, probably under the name *girasole articiocco* meaning "sunflower artichoke". It is thought that girasole got corrupted to "Jerusalem", while the similarity of flavour to the artichoke gave it the second part of its name. The Chinese artichoke came to us only recently, late in the 19th century. Its other name, *crosnes*, is derived from the small town in France where they were first grown in Europe.

To prepare a globe artichoke, first trim off the top third-to-a-half of the leaves (as only the bases of the leaves have any flesh attached to them), then peel away the outside layer of leaves (which have little attached flesh). You can go on removing all the leaves to make a cup, as described on page 99 or cook the artichokes with the remaining leaves in place for them to be consumed at the table.

Cook the artichokes upside down in simmering salted water acidulated with lemon juice (to keep them from discolouring), covered with a plate or lid from a smaller pan to keep them totally submerged, until the base is tender to the point of a knife. The small inner leaves and the hairy choke in the centre are then also removed (using a teaspoon or melon baller) to reveal the flat disc of delicious heart at the base.

The whole artichokes are then presented at the table for diners to pick off the leaves one by one and scrape off the flesh at their base between their teeth. Melted butter, vinaigrette, hollandaise, etc. are usually served with it so that the leaves can first be dunked in the dressing. When we make cups out of artichokes and there are lots of flesh-tipped leaves left over, we deep-fry them for a delicious and unusual party snack.

The two other types, being tubers, just need washing or peeling and simmering in boiling salted water or stock until tender. Both can, however, be used raw in salads if grated or sliced very thinly.

All three artichokes do have an unusual feature in common other than their wonderful nutty flavour. Most of their carbohydrates are in the form of inulin, a starch which the body cannot use for energy but which does help nourish the good bacteria in the gut and stabilize blood sugar levels. The down side of this is evidenced by the obvious flatulence all three types of vegetable evince, as the body finds it so difficult to break inulin down. Globe artichokes are said to help lower blood cholesterol and Jerusalem artichokes are every bit as packed with iron as meat.

Caesar Salad

The capers are important in this dish as they take the place of the classic anchovies. Try those packed in salt rather than immersed in brine, as their flavour is far superior.

SERVES 4

2-3 drops white wine vinegar
2 eggs
1 tbsp French mustard
150ml (5fl oz) extra virgin olive oil
100g (3½oz) Parmesan, grated, plus
  more shaved Parmesan to garnish
2 garlic cloves, finely chopped

150g (5½oz) capers
150ml (5fl oz) sunflower oil
salt and black pepper
juice of ½ lemon
1 large baby cos lettuce or
  2 little gems
about 20 pitted black olives

CROÛTONS
2-3 tbsp olive oil
2-3 garlic cloves, finely chopped
few sprigs of rosemary,
  finely chopped
1 small baguette, cut into cubes

1 | Preheat the oven to 190°C/375°F/gas mark 5. Bring a small pan of water, with a few drops of white wine vinegar, to the boil and carefully crack the eggs into the water. Poach gently for 1 minute only and then drain through a sieve.

2 | When well drained, transfer the eggs to a food processor and add the mustard. Start the machine running and slowly trickle in all but 2-3 tbsp of the olive oil as if making mayonnaise. Stop the machine and add the grated Parmesan, garlic and two-thirds of the capers. Start the machine again, then trickle in the sunflower oil. Process until everything is nicely mixed. Season to taste with salt and pepper and add the lemon juice.

3 | To make the croûtons, heat the olive oil and fry the garlic and rosemary briefly. Add the bread cubes and stir well to coat. Scatter on a baking sheet and bake for about 10 minutes, until nicely browned and crisp, shaking from time to time.

4 | Tear the lettuce into a large salad bowl, add the olives and sprinkle with the remaining extra virgin olive oil (this helps them take on a coating of the thickish dressing). Spoon over the Caesar dressing and toss well to coat thoroughly, adding the croûtons at the last minute so they are not all coated.

Thai Noodle Salad

The main reason for the inclusion of this recipe is that we just love the clean zingy flavours of Thai food.

SERVES 4

350g (12oz) rice vermicelli
150g (5½oz) each of baby sweetcorn, carrots and mange tout
1 red pepper, seeded
5-6 spring onions
100g (3½oz) beansprouts
bunch of coriander, separated into whole leaves

DRESSING

knob of fresh root ginger
1 red chilli, seeded
2 lemongrass stalks
5 tbsp sesame oil
1 tbsp sugar
juice of 2 limes
good splash of soy sauce

1 | Well ahead if possible (so the flavours can get friendly), make the dressing. Cut the ginger into fine julienne strips. Cut the chilli across into halves and then into julienne strips. Discard the hard outer leaves of the lemongrass, and chop only the soft inner parts. Mix all the dressing ingredients together in a bowl.

2 | To make the salad, prepare the rice vermicelli by soaking them as per the packet instructions and drain well.

3 | Quarter the baby sweetcorn lengthwise. Peel off all the outside of the carrots to leave just the paler core, then pare into strips. Cut the mange tout lengthwise into three. Cut the red pepper into julienne strips. Cut the spring onions across into 5cm (2in) lengths, and then in half to make julienne strips.

4 | In a large salad bowl, mix the noodles with all the other salad ingredients. Pour over the dressing and toss to coat everything with it.

Hot and Spicy Main Courses

One thing that we have found as vegetarians is that when eating out, lots of the "main courses" on restaurant menus are nothing more than large portions of starters, and for that reason tend to pall after a few mouthfuls. Our philosophy is that main-course dishes should offer considerable variety on the plate. Cooking lots of little things that work together beautifully is part of our culture, and we know from customers' comments that this diversity has played a considerable part in the success of our menus.

Another contributory element to that success has been our bold and imaginative spicing. It's second nature to us, but we still have to guide even some of our most ardent and regular fans into it gently as they have suffered at the hands of slapdash Indian and Malaysian restaurant kitchens, playing to the macho culture of "how hot can you take it?".

You will see that some of our dishes in this chapter are indeed super-hot, such as the mushroom chatani on page 115, using lots of chillies – seeds and all. In the context of that dish, though, it works perfectly and produces a balanced dish that doesn't offend even the most sensitive of palates. Elsewhere, our use of chilli heat is much more moderate, and you can always adjust the chilli quantity up or down according to taste.

Root Vegetable Tagine
with Pickled Baby Lemons and Pomegranate Salsa

We love this rich, spicy, aromatic and fruity dish, which is almost as comforting to cook as it is to eat. The tagine is one of those classic dishes that we always wanted to re-create for vegetarians.

SERVES 4-6

2 cinnamon sticks
1½ tsp cloves
3 tbsp coriander seeds
a little olive oil
1 tbsp ground turmeric
1 large Spanish onion, finely chopped
100g (3½oz) grated fresh root
  ginger, grated
1 red chilli, seeded and chopped
6 garlic cloves, crushed

1½-2 x 400g tins chopped tomatoes
100g (3½oz) dried dates, puréed
1 sweet potato, halved and sliced
  at an angle
2 fennel bulbs, cut into batons
  about 1cm (½in) thick and 2-2.5cm
  (¾-1in) long
1 celeriac root, cut into batons
  as above
150g (5½oz) fresh spinach leaves

handful of coriander leaves, chopped
1 recipe quantity couscous
  (page 209), to serve
pickled lemons (page 113), to serve
pomegranate salsa (page 184), to
  serve

1 | Toast the cinnamon sticks, cloves and coriander seeds in a dry frying pan until their aroma rises. Grind finely using a mortar and pestle (or a coffee grinder). This preliminary exercise is well worth the trouble as the flavours and aromas of the spices really come to life compared to those of pre-ground spices.

2 | Heat a little olive oil in a heavy-based saucepan and stir the spices, including the ground turmeric, in it briefly. Add the onion and sauté for a few minutes, then add the ginger, chilli and garlic. Turn the heat down and simmer for 10-15 minutes, until the flavours are well blended. Add the tomatoes, dates and all the vegetables except the spinach. Cover the pan and simmer gently for 40 minutes.

3 | Fold the spinach and coriander into the vegetable tagine, season to taste and arrange on plates. Put mounds of the couscous to the side on each plate and sit two to three pickled baby lemons on top of the couscous. Splash the pomegranate salsa around each plate.

1
 | 2
  | 3

Pickled Lemons

Pickled or preserved lemons are common all over the Arab world, but most particularly in North Africa, as a flavouring and condiment. The skins of the lemons so treated develop a silky texture and what Claudia Roden calls a "curious and wonderfully intense flavour" that works well against spicy food, but also adds character to all sorts of dishes. Sometimes also flavoured with coriander seeds, cinnamon and cloves, pickled lemons are also delicious in salads and have become a valued "secret ingredient" among many of today's chefs.

Pickled lemons can be bought bottled or canned in good delicatessens or ethnic food stores, but you can quite easily make your own.

1 | Scrub about 18 uncoated baby lemons (if you can't get baby lemons, use thick-skinned large ones) and then score the skins deeply all over.

2 | Put in a non-reactive dish, cover with rock salt and try to work it into the lemons.

3 | Pack them into a jar as tightly as possible and add lemon juice to cover. Seal tightly and leave in a cool place for two to three weeks, giving the jar a shake and turning it upside-down every few days.

The pickling liquid also takes on an oily consistency, so you can use it in dressings or drizzle it directly on salads, fish sauces, etc. You can do the same with limes to equal effect.

Some people speed up the process by quartering the lemons – indeed Chris and Carolyn Caldicott in their redoubtable *World Food Café Cookbook* recommend just blanching lemon quarters for a minute, then refreshing them, for an instant (if inauthentic) substitute to the real thing, should you be caught without preserved lemons to hand.

Falia Bargi
(Dry green bean "curry")

This is a dish our Gran made for us when we first became vegetarian. For the real experience use Indian beans, but you will have to cook them for longer – 40-45 minutes. Our uncle used to say "first take your children home and then give them one kind of bargi", which we thought meant a good hiding, but now we think he meant something nutritious they will enjoy!

SERVES 4

250g (9oz) green beans, cut into 2cm (¾in) lengths
200g (7oz) new potatoes
2-3 tomatoes, chopped
salt and black pepper
bunch of coriander, chopped
parathas **(page 82), to serve (optional)**

"CURRY" MIX
2 tbsp vegetable oil
1 tbsp each of panch phoran and garam masala
5-6 whole cloves
large chunk of fresh root ginger, finely chopped
3-4 garlic cloves, finely chopped

2 green chillies, seeded and finely chopped
1 large onion, finely chopped

CARDAMOM RICE
1 cup basmati rice
splash of vegetable oil
2 cardamom pods, crushed

1 | First make the "curry" mix: heat the oil in a wok or large heavy-based pan and stir-fry the spices over a fairly high heat until their aromas rise. Lower the heat and stir in the ginger, garlic, chillies and onion. Sweat for a few minutes until these are softened.

2 | Add the beans and stir to coat, followed by the potatoes and chopped tomatoes. Season with some salt and pepper. Cover and cook gently for about 25 minutes, until the potatoes are just tender. Remove the lid to let the dish dry out a little and cook for 5-10 minutes more until what we call the *hakakah* starts to develop, i.e. the mixture is just catching on the bottom of the pan to form a nicely caramelized (and tasty) crust, which we all used to fight for.

3 | Meanwhile, prepare the rice. Rinse the rice in a colander until the water runs clear. Heat the oil in a heavy-based pan, stir in the cardamom and cook for about 1 minute. Stir in the rice until it is well coated. Add 2 cups of water, bring to the boil, lower the heat and cover tightly. Cook over the gentlest of heats for about 20 minutes, until all the water has been absorbed and the rice grains are just tender but still firm to the bite.

4 | Finish the *bargi* by stirring in the coriander and adjusting the seasoning to taste. Serve with the rice, fluffed up with a fork, and/or *parathas*.

Mushroom Chatani

Our Gran's *chatani* were legendary. Usually based on chicken, these dry, sour curries were so fiercely hot that we kids were given just about a spoonful of them with a whole bowl of rice. When our parents came over on the boat from India, they were really worried that there would be no *kosher* food and they wouldn't be able to eat anything on board, so they brought with them a milk churn filled with *chatani*. They would get rice from the ship's kitchen and have the *chatani* with this for every meal.

SERVES 4

1 large Spanish onion
5cm (2in) chunk fresh root ginger
6-7 garlic cloves
3-4 tbsp vegetable oil
4-5 green chillies, chopped
2 tbsp each of garam masala
 and ground cumin

75g (2¾oz) tamarind concentrate
4 tomatoes, skinned and chopped
 (or a 400g tin chopped tomatoes)
good dollop of tomato purée
2 tbsp sugar
6 curry leaves

500g (18oz) button mushrooms,
 halved or quartered
plain boiled basmati rice, to serve

1 | Purée the onion in a blender, add the ginger and garlic and purée again.

2 | Heat the oil in a large heavy pan until good and hot and add the chillies. Stir for 30 seconds or so, add the garam masala, cumin and tamarind, and cook for about 1 minute. Then stir in the onion mix and simmer for 15-20 minutes until everything is well cooked and amalgamated.

3 | Add the tomatoes, tomato purée, sugar and curry leaves. Cover and simmer for a further 30 minutes.

4 | Add the mushrooms and cook for 10 minutes more, uncovered for the last 5 minutes to let the dish dry off a bit. Serve with plain boiled white rice.

Middle Eastern Platter

The secrets of good falafel are ensuring that the chickpeas are processed until fine and that the mix is thick enough to be moulded in spoons, and frying for just long enough for the chickpeas to cook through. The brine pickling for the pickled vegetables also works with cucumbers, while the vinegar method for the okra suits celery, carrots and cauliflower. We like to make tabbouleh in the Lebanese way – lots of herb and little couscous.

SERVES 6-8

PICKLED VEGETABLES
4 turnips or 2 whole *kohlrabi*,
  halved and cut into half-moons
  about 5mm (¼in) thick
1 small beetroot, halved and
  cut as above
1 garlic clove, bruised
4 heaped tbsp sea salt

PICKLED OKRA
8-10 okra
3 garlic cloves, thinly sliced
2.5cm (1in) piece fresh root ginger,
  thinly sliced
150ml (5fl oz) white wine vinegar
2 whole red chillies
4 tbsp sugar

PITTA BREAD
pinch of sugar
about ½ tsp active dry yeast
300g (10½oz) plain flour
2 tbsp onion seeds or sesame seeds
several good splashes of olive oil

1 | Four or five days ahead, prepare the pickled vegetables. Mix the vegetables with the garlic and salt, pack into a jar and just cover with water. Put a lid on, cover and leave in a warm place for four to five days. (At home we would leave them on the window sill where they'd get the sun.) After this time you can keep what you don't use in the refrigerator.

1 | Also several days ahead, prepare the pickled okra. Halve the okra across and split each half in two lengthways, but don't cut all the way through. Stuff the okra halves with the garlic and ginger and pack into a jar. Bring the vinegar to the boil with the chillies and sugar. Allow to cool, then pour over the stuffed okra. Leave for about three to four days. The okra will come out nice and crunchy, and the garlic and ginger will have lovely unusual flavours (still quite full on).

1 | Mix about 100ml (3½fl oz) of water with the sugar and yeast in a small bowl, and leave for about 5 minutes until beginning to bubble up. Sift the flour into a bowl and add the yeast mixture and seeds, then add a little more flour or water as appropriate to keep the dough moist and elastic. Knead on a well-floured surface for about 10 minutes. Lightly oil the dough, put it in a bowl, cover and leave for about 1 hour to prove.

2 | When ready to serve the platter, knock back the proved dough for a few minutes and then roll into eight small balls. Roll each ball into a flat round about 3mm (⅛in) thick and drizzle with a little olive oil. Get a dry pan good and hot and fry the pittas one at a time for 2 minutes on each side, until nicely coloured and puffed.

FALAFEL

200g (7oz) chickpeas, soaked overnight in cold water
1 large onion, chopped
large handful of coriander
1 tbsp ground coriander
2-3 garlic cloves, chopped
1 tsp garam masala
2 tbsp white sesame seeds
pinch of baking soda
1 green chilli, seeded
2 spring onions, chopped
juice of ½ lemon
1 tsp paprika
salt to taste
handful of couscous (optional)
vegetable oil, for frying

BABA GHANOUSH

2 aubergines
a little extra virgin olive oil, plus more to dress
1 tbsp roasted garlic (page 212)
drizzle of tahini
few sprigs of mint
few sprigs of coriander, plus more to garnish

FALIA BIRZIT (GREEN BEANS IN TOMATO AND HERB SAUCE)

good splash of olive oil
1 small onion, finely chopped
3-4 garlic cloves, finely chopped
1 x 400g can chopped tomatoes
good handful each of coriander and mint leaves, chopped
few drops of lemon juice
salt to taste
250g (9oz) green beans

---

1 | To make the falafel, drain the chickpeas and cook in fresh boiling water for about 40 minutes, until quite soft (as with all pulses, cook a little longer than when they first feel soft in the hot water as they harden up again when they cool). Drain. Process the chickpeas with all the other ingredients until smooth. If too wet, add a handful of couscous (you are aiming for a softish paste). Leave for an hour for the chickpeas to absorb the moisture.

2 | To cook the falafel, mould the mixture into large walnut-sized balls and flatten them slightly. Get oil for deep-frying really hot in a wok or deep-frying pan and add the falafel in batches of three to four at a time. Turn the heat down slightly and cook for 3-4 minutes on each side.

1 | To make the baba ghanoush, preheat the oven to 180°C/350°F/gas mark 4. Roast the aubergines whole over a naked flame until blackened and blistering all over. When cool enough to handle, peel off the skin, trying to catch any juices as you go, and carefully remove any burned bits of flesh. Lightly brush the peeled aubergines with oil and roast in a greaseproof paper-lined baking tray for 20 minutes, until softened. Leave to cool.

2 | Process this with all the other ingredients (including any juices captured while peeling) until smooth. To serve, drizzle with a little extra virgin olive oil and garnish with coriander leaves.

1 | To make the falia birzit, heat the oil in a frying pan and sweat the onion until translucent. Add the garlic and cook for 2-3 minutes more. Add the tomatoes with their liquid, bring to a simmer and cook gently for about 10 minutes. Stir in the chopped coriander and mint, with a few drops of lemon juice and salt to taste.

2 | In a separate pan, blanch the beans in boiling salted water for 1 minute, drain and add to the tomato sauce. Cook for 3-4 minutes, then leave to cool and sprinkle with more oil to serve.

continued...

Middle Eastern Platter

(continued)

HUMMUS
100g (3½oz) chickpeas, soaked
  overnight in cold water
1 tbsp tahini
4 tbsp extra virgin olive oil,
  plus more to drizzle
1 or 2 garlic cloves
juice of 1 lemon
salt and pepper
paprika, to garnish (optional)
coriander sprigs to garnish
  (optional)

TABBOULEH
about 2-3 tbsp *burghul* **or**
  ready-prepared couscous
juice of 2 lemons
55g (2oz) each of mint, parsley
  and coriander leaves,
finely chopped, plus more whole
  leaves to garnish
2 tomatoes, seeds and pulp
  discarded and flesh finely diced
3 spring onions, finely chopped
3 tbsp olive oil
salt

TO SERVE
red schoog (page 193)

1 | To prepare the hummus, drain the chickpeas and cook in fresh boiling water for about 40 minutes, until quite soft (as with all pulses, cook a little longer than when they first feel soft in the hot water as they harden up again when they cool). Drain, reserving the cooking water. In a blender, purée the drained chickpeas and then whiz in the remaining ingredients. Add just enough of the reserved cooking liquid to get the right texture of a thick paste. Adjust the seasoning with salt, pepper and more lemon juice if necessary. Drizzle with more olive oil, sprinkle with paprika and garnish with coriander sprigs to serve.

1 | To make the tabbouleh, make up the *burghul* or couscous by soaking it in the lemon juice. When just tender, mix in all the rest of the ingredients with salt to taste. Garnish with a few whole mint, parsley and coriander leaves.

To serve, set out all the dishes and the schoog in separate bowls for people to serve themselves.

Cajun Aubergine

Dare we say it, this dish of aubergine deep-fried with Cajun spices is slightly reminiscent of southern fried chicken – but really nice. The spiciness and texture contrast make it very satisfying.

SERVES 4

2 large aubergines
vegetable oil, for deep-frying
about 16 okra
good pinch of Cajun spice seasoning
handful of coriander leaves
few drops of lemon juice
1 fennel bulb, cored and cut into
** julienne strips**
1-2 sweet potatoes, cut at an
** angle into long slices**

olive oil, for brushing
bean salsa (page 187), to serve

COATING

55g (2oz) plain flour
3 tbsp Cajun spice seasoning
1 egg, beaten
dash of milk
200g (7oz) dry breadcrumbs

1 | Peel and halve the aubergines widthways and hollow them out, leaving a 6-8mm (about ⅜in) thick shell.

2 | For the coating, mix the flour and spice together in a bowl. Beat the egg and milk together, pour into a separate bowl and put the breadcrumbs on a plate.

3 | Heat the oil for deep-frying until almost smoking. Dip each aubergine half in the flour mixed with the spice, then in the egg-and-milk mixture and finally in the breadcrumbs, shaking off excess each time. Deep-fry for 4-5 minutes, turning if necessary, until golden all over. Drain on kitchen paper, upright rather than on their sides so they keep their shapes. Set aside.

4 | Heat some vegetable oil in a wok or frying pan and fry the okra with half the spices and half the coriander leaves, until the okra is just softened – about 5 minutes. Stir in the lemon juice and set aside to cool slightly.

5 | Cook the fennel in exactly the same way with the remaining spices and coriander.

6 | Brush the sweet potato slices with oil and griddle, grill or fry until tender and nicely coloured.

7 | Arrange the sweet potato slices overlapping in flower petal shapes on each of four serving plates. Stuff the aubergine shells with the okra and fennel (standing them up looks dramatic) and set one on each bed of sweet potato. Place spoonfuls of the bean salsa in-between the sweet potato petals.

Teriyaki Aubergine

The stimulus for this dish was wanting to use horseradish in an unusual way. The parallels with wasabi led us towards Japanese flavours.

SERVES 4
about 3 large aubergines, cut lengthways into 12 slices about 5mm (¼in) thick
salt
coriander pesto (page 180)
4 large plum tomatoes, thinly sliced
55g (2oz) brown breadcrumbs
100g (3½oz) toasted sesame seeds

HORSERADISH FILLING
50ml (2fl oz) sesame oil
55g (2oz) each of fresh horseradish and fresh root ginger, grated
5 garlic cloves, finely chopped
50ml (2fl oz) *mirin* (sweet rice wine)

TERIYAKI SAUCE
3 tbsp sesame oil
4 lemongrass stalks, chopped
55g (2oz) fresh root ginger, finely chopped
10 lime leaves
1 red chilli, seeded and chopped
150ml (5fl oz) light soy sauce
5 tbsp honey
50ml (2fl oz) *mirin*
2 tbsp cornflour, dissolved in a little cold water

NOODLES
300g (10½oz) egg noodles
3 tbsp sesame oil
1 tbsp finely chopped root ginger
handful of coriander leaves, chopped

GARNISH (OPTIONAL)
fresh shiitake mushrooms, sautéed lightly in a little butter and olive oil
2 pak choi, halved and char-grilled briefly on the flat side then dressed with a little soy sauce and lime juice
baby sweetcorn, trimmed
mange tout, trimmed

1 | Salt the aubergine slices generously and allow to stand for 30 minutes. Rinse well and pat dry with kitchen paper. Roast on a char-grill or griddle until lightly coloured and beginning to turn translucent.

2 | To make the horseradish filling, heat the sesame oil in a wok, add all the other ingredients except the *mirin* and sauté for 12 minutes, stirring continuously. Add the *mirin* at the end and set aside.

3 | To make the *teriyaki* sauce, heat the sesame oil in a wok and sauté the lemongrass, ginger, lime leaves and chilli. Add the soy sauce and honey, bring to the boil, then simmer for 20 minutes. Add the *mirin*, thicken with the cornflour mixture and pass through a sieve. If the sauce tastes too salty, dilute it with 3 or 4 tbsp water.

4 | Preheat the oven to 180°C/350°F/gas mark 4. For each person, layer three slices of aubergine, spreading the first with the horseradish mixture, the second with the coriander pesto and arranging the tomato slices on that, then topping with the third slice of aubergine. Coat with breadcrumbs and sesame seeds and bake for 15-20 minutes.

5 | Cook the noodles in boiling water until just tender. Drain. Heat the sesame oil in a wok, add the ginger and coriander, then toss in the drained noodles. Stir-fry until coated with the spicy oil.

6 | Place the aubergine layers on a bed of noodles, drizzle with the *teriyaki* sauce and, if you like, garnish with fresh shiitake mushrooms and wilted pak choi, mange tout and baby sweetcorn.

Pad Thai

The unashamed reason for this dish being on our menu is that we want to cook vegetables and make dishes that we love. We love to create vegetarian versions of classic dishes, and we devised this for one of our fungi fests, with lovely subtly flavoured chicken-of-the-woods and grifola mushrooms instead of the tofu or seitan.

SERVES 4

350g (12oz) flat rice noodles
 (rice sticks)
150g (5½oz) baby sweetcorn
150g (5½oz) mange touts
150g (5½oz) shiitake or oyster
 mushrooms
250g (9oz) firm tofu or chunks
 of seitan (page 73)

3 tbsp sesame oil
5-6 spring onions, cut at an
 angle into 5mm (¼in) slices
1 head pak choi
4 tbsp Thai red curry paste (page 183)
2 tbsp sugar
100g (3½oz) beansprouts
bunch of coriander, chopped

100g (3½oz) toasted peanuts,
 crushed
juice of ½-1 lime
good splash of soy sauce

1 | Prepare the noodles by putting them in a bowl and covering them with boiling water. Leave to steep for about 5 minutes and then drain and cover with cold water.

2 | Cut the baby sweetcorn and mange touts across at an angle into three or four pieces. Slice or tear the mushrooms thinly. Cube the tofu or seitan and fry briefly in 1 tbsp of the sesame oil until crisp. Cut the spring onions at an angle into 5mm (1¼in) slices. Shred the pak choi.

3 | Heat the remaining sesame oil in a wok or large frying pan until very hot and stir-fry the curry paste briefly. Stir in the sugar, then stir-fry the vegetables, adding them in the order of firmness and stirring well between each addition, starting with the corn and mushrooms followed by the tofu or seitan, the mange touts and spring onions and then the pak choi. Drain the noodles well, toss them in and finish with the beansprouts, coriander and nuts.

4 | Taste and add lime and soy sauce to taste. The lime juice should balance out the sugar (you may have to add a little more sugar for a good sweet-and-sour balance). Serve immediately.

Red Thai Vegetable Curry

The virtue of this particular curry is that you can use almost any combination of vegetables in season, but try to get a good mix of texture and colours.

SERVES 4

½ recipe quantity Thai red curry
 paste (page 183)
1 tbsp each of ground coriander,
 paprika, ground cumin and
turmeric
600ml (1 pint) coconut milk
2 tbsp tomato purée or puréed
 sun-dried tomatoes
1 tbsp palm or brown sugar
1 tbsp chopped fresh lime leaves

salt
500g (18oz) mixed vegetables,
 ideally including broccoli, baby
 sweetcorn, red peppers,
 mange tout, carrots, pak choi and
 shiitake mushrooms
olive oil
steamed Thai fragrant rice,
 to serve
pineapple salsa (page 186), to serve

1 | In a large heavy-based pan, mix the curry paste, spices, coconut milk, tomato purée, sugar and lime leaves. Bring to the boil, lower the heat and simmer for 30 minutes, until reduced by about one-sixth to a sauce-like consistency.

2 | Meanwhile, prepare the vegetables. Blanch the broccoli in boiling salted water for a minute, drain and, when cool enough to handle, break into florets. Halve the pepper(s), seed, cut into strips and sauté lightly in a little olive oil. Halve the sweetcorn and mange tout at an angle; cut the carrot(s) into strips; slice the pak choi lengthwise, and halve or slice the shiitake if large.

3 | Add all the prepared vegetables to the pan of sauce, stir in well and cook gently for 2-3 minutes to warm through.

4 | Mound the rice in four serving bowls, spoon over the curry and serve the pineapple salsa separately.

Kassa

(Burmese cold noodle salad with hot curry sauce)

As we Indo-Iraqis have settled as far east as Burma, we have Burmese relatives who cook this dish. The curry paste would be different – certainly without the galangal. We've suggested hard-boiled egg as a garnish, but you might like to try baking the eggs in a low oven for a few hours; this gives their insides a brown colour and gives them an interesting flavour.

SERVES 4

250g (9oz) fine egg noodles
few drops of sesame oil
500g (18oz) mixed vegetables –
  at least 4 of the following: broccoli,
  mange touts, baby sweetcorn,
  courgette, mooli radish, seeded
  red peppers and carrots – all cut
  into long strips

HOT CURRY SAUCE
1 star anise
1 tbsp cumin seeds, ground
1 tbsp ground turmeric
½ recipe quantity Thai red curry
  paste (page 183)
1 large onion, finely chopped
1 large tin coconut milk
2 lime leaves
handful of coriander leaves, chopped

juice of ½ lime
salt

GARNISHES
2 hard-boiled eggs, mashed
chopped spring onion
mixed roasted nuts and seeds
caramelized garlic slices
chopped chillies
fried diced tofu

1 | Ideally, make the sauce at least 2-3 hours ahead or even the day before, to let the flavours develop. In a dry pan, toast the star anise and cumin seeds until their aroma rises. Add the turmeric and Thai red curry paste and stir-fry for 3-4 minutes. Stir in the onion and cook over a low heat until that softens. If it looks at any time like it is going to catch, add a splash or two of water.

2 | Stir in the coconut milk (the consistency of coconut milk varies considerably – if it is very thick use only three-quarters of the can and make up the rest with water). Bring back to a simmer, stir in the lime leaves and leave to simmer and reduce for about 20 minutes. About halfway through that time, stir in the coriander. Finish with the lime juice and salt to taste. Keep warm.

3 | Cook the noodles according to packet instructions. Drain in a colander, rinse with cold water to stop them cooking, then drain well again and stir in some sesame oil to coat them. If you wish, deep-fry a large handful of them in vegetable oil in a wok as an extra garnish.

4 | Blanch the vegetables for 1 minute in boiling water, refresh in cold water, drain and pat dry.

5 | Pile the soft noodles on the plates, and arrange the veg decoratively on top of them. Spoon over the warm sauce and top with some fried noodles if you have made them. Either arrange the garnishes around the plate or serve in separate small bowls.

Rolled Tortillas

This is our take on Mexican food, as we long ago discovered that you can't get decent Mexican food in London. Some of the ingredients don't seem very Mexican though, as in the leap of invention it became more about using the presentation to combine unusual flavours. Don't cut the sweet potatoes too small or they will disintegrate as they cook.

SERVES 4

8 wheat or corn tortillas
1 x 400g can chopped tomatoes or
 2 large tomatoes, skinned and
 chopped
1 tbsp olive oil
1 tsp pasilla black bean salsa
 (page 187), plus more to serve
guacamole (page 208), to serve
soured cream, to serve

BEETROOT AND FETA FILLING
500g (18oz) beetroot, peeled
 and diced
a little vegetable oil
salt and black pepper
1 large onion, finely chopped
2-3 garlic cloves, finely chopped
handful of mint
½ bunch coriander, chopped
juice of 1 lemon
200g (7oz) feta cheese, cut into cubes

SWEET POTATO FILLING
500g (18oz) sweet potatoes, cut into
 largish dice
good pinch of ground coriander
1 corn cob
½ bunch coriander, chopped
bunch of spring onions, chopped
1 tsp caster sugar
juice of 1 lime

1 | A couple of hours ahead, preheat the oven to 150°C/300°F/gas mark 2. Toss the beetroot for the beetroot and feta filling in a little vegetable oil to coat, together with some salt and pepper. Spread out on a baking tray, cover with foil and roast for about 1½ hours, until the pieces just give when pressed. Remove the foil for the last 10 minutes or so to dry the beetroot off.

2 | Increase the oven setting to 200°C/400°F/gas mark 6. Toss the sweet potatoes in a little vegetable oil to coat, together with the ground coriander and salt and some black pepper. Spread out on a baking tray and roast for 15-20 minutes, until the pieces just give when pressed.

3 | Griddle the corn over a high heat until nicely coloured all over. When cool enough to handle, cut off the kernels by standing it on end and cutting down around the core with a stout sharp knife.

4 | To finish the beetroot and feta filling, in a large heavy-based pan, heat a little oil and cook the onion and garlic until nicely softened. Stir in the mint, coriander and lemon juice, then fold in the beetroot and feta. Spoon one-third of the mixture into the food processor and blend to a purée. Stir that back into the filling to give it body and coherence. Adjust the seasoning if necessary.

5 | To finish the sweet potato filling, in a large bowl, mix the sweet potato and corn kernels, then stir in the coriander, spring onions, sugar and lime juice. Adjust the seasoning if necessary.

6 | Heat the tortillas in a dry pan until nicely flexible and slightly puffed up.

7 | Mix the tomatoes with the olive oil and the tsp of pasilla black bean salsa. Spread this over the tortillas, then fill half with each filling and fold up. Serve one of each on a serving plate, either with a dollop each of pasilla black bean salsa, guacamole and soured cream alongside or serve these accompaniments in separate bowls for people to help themselves.

Beetroot
(Beta vulgaris)

Until lately rather overlooked, the beetroot is one of those vegetables we like to bring back to a wider audience. In Britain, unfortunately, most people's experience of beetroot has been restricted to the pickled root version. Only in the last few years has it been possible to buy them raw and untreated from anything but the best markets and greengrocers, and pick-your-owns.

There is an apocryphal story about how the beetroot got its name, which we think will appeal to vegetarians. The profuse bleeding of red liquid that follows beetroot being cut led it to being called *la bête* or "the beast". As long as it is carefully controlled, though, that lovely colour can give drama to all sorts of dishes.

In both the Arab and Indian cultures, the beet plant is much more valued for its tasty leaves than its roots – it is, after all, a member of the same *chenopodiaceae* (goose foot) family as spinach, chard and fashionable quinoa. Arab food does, however, have beetroot salads and the Indians enjoy beetroot raitas, but, as far as we can gather, it was the Germanic tribes who first cultivated the plant mainly for its roots in the Middle Ages.

As you can see in the Soups chapter, though, we grew up with a vivid borscht-like beetroot soup at the heart of our family cuisine, with just the *kubba* or spiced dumplings in it declaring a difference. It only occurred to us recently that this soup must have come to us from Eastern Europe via the third pillar of Indo-Iraqi culture, the Jewish dimension.

As you can imagine, the idea of boiling beetroot was an anathema to us, so instinctively we roasted them – a technique that has become fashionable, as it really brings out the full earthy flavour of the vegetable. As we do with other roots such as the spud, we sometimes roast them in their skins (at 160°C/325°F/gas mark 3 for about 2-2½ hours), which helps retain all their flavour and nutrients. We skin them while they are still warm, as it is easier to do then. Lately, however, we have taken to dicing the skinned raw roots, tossing them in a little oil and roasting them in a baking tray covered with foil. This way they steam as much as roast, and give superb results, particularly if you are going to purée them.

When you are buying beetroot, look for those with a good deep colour, as this usually indicates nice long unforced growth, and don't get any that are too large or have too much leaf scarring around the tops as these are usually tough and fibrous. Store them upright in a cool dry place and, when you have to, twist off the tops rather than cutting them as this helps minimize bleeding of the juices.

Beetroot takes well to a wide range of flavourings, from fruit such as oranges and apples to pungent aromatics such as onions, garlic, mustard and horseradish. In a salad they really suit the nut oils in the dressing. They are at their very best with really simple treatments, such as a touch of lemon juice or melted butter and some black pepper.

Corn Cakes
with Pacific Chilli Vegetables

This spicy version of grilled veg makes a lovely summer dish; we created it as a means of making the most of the lovely subtle flavour of the chipotle chilli.

SERVES 4

CORN CAKES
1 corn cob
2 lime leaves, stalks removed
good bunch of coriander
good sprig of thyme
1 red chilli, seeded and finely
** chopped**
100g (3½oz) polenta
vegetable oil, for frying

DRESSING
1 red romano (long pointed sweet)
** pepper**
2 chipotle chillies (smoked
** jalapeños), soaked if dried**
juice of 1 orange and 1 lime
sprig of coriander
about 5 tbsp olive oil

VEGETABLES
8 baby artichokes, prepared and
** hearts removed, as described on**
** page 102, then halved**
top half of a butternut squash,
** peeled, cut down into halves and**
** cut into 3mm-thick half moons**

1 large aubergine, cut into rounds
** about 1cm (½in) thick**
1 courgette, cut lengthwise on a
** mandolin grater into thick ribbons**
1 fennel bulb, cored and cut into
** wedges**

TO SERVE
black bean salsa (page 187)

1 | Griddle the corn over a high heat until nicely coloured all over. When cool enough to handle, cut off the kernels by standing it on end and cutting down around the core with a stout sharp knife.

2 | To prepare the corn cakes, roughly chop the corn kernels. In a saucepan, heat 200ml (7fl oz) water with the herbs, chilli and corn, then add the polenta and mix well. Using an 8cm (3¼in) pastry cutter, mould into four cakes. Chill for 40 minutes to set.

3 | While the cakes chill, make the dressing. Roast and skin the romano pepper. Purée the flesh with the chillies, then blend in the citrus juices and coriander with just enough olive oil to make a spreadable mixture.

4 | To cook the vegetables, brush them all with the dressing and griddle until tender and nicely coloured.

5 | Heat the vegetable oil in a frying pan and fry the chilled corn cakes for 4-5 minutes on each side, until nicely browned and crisp.

6 | Arrange with the roasted veg and bean salsa.

Milder Main Courses

I suppose you could call this the "More Mediterranean Main Course" chapter, although one of the most classically Med of dishes, our ratatouille, does include a chilli for added kick. This chapter certainly draws more on European culinary traditions than on those of the Middle, Near and Far East.

Nevertheless, even here we try to offer as much variety on the plate as possible. It is more difficult to do this with many Mediterranean dishes, including pastas and risottos, but we still try to ensure that every mouthful offers the chance to explore unusual combinations that present the palate with a flavour adventure.

With only about a dozen vegetables to draw on, we had to look for intriguing ways to present them so that not only could their flavour be appreciated, but also their potential explored through great pairings with other ingredients to create taste and texture contrasts in a dish.

The watchwords in our kitchen have always been "taste", "texture" and "colour". As well as making a good presentation, this last is really important, as any nutritionist will tell you, because a good variety of plant colour on the plate means a good range of nutrients.

Stonehenge Veg

This "signature dish" came about because we are obsessed with stuffing vegetables and finding new ways of presenting them.

SERVES 4
2 green courgettes, 12cm (4½in) long
2 yellow courgettes, 12cm (4½in) long
oil, for brushing
salt and black pepper
4 each of baby aubergines, large
  ceps and tomatoes

GREEN COURGETTE STUFFING
40g (1½oz) green lentils
1 tbsp olive oil
2 shallots, finely chopped
2 garlic cloves, finely chopped
1 tomato, skinned, seeded and diced
handful of basil leaves, shredded
splash of red wine

YELLOW COURGETTE STUFFING
30g (1¼oz) sun-dried tomatoes,
  drained
100g (3½oz) ricotta cheese
25g (1oz) Parmesan cheese, grated

AUBERGINE STUFFING
55g (2oz) butter
400g (14oz) mature spinach, thick
  stems and veins removed
100g (3½oz) soft rindless goat's cheese

CEP STUFFING
knob of butter
sprig of rosemary, chopped

handful of parsley leaves, chopped
40g (1½oz) fresh breadcrumbs

TOMATO STUFFING
1 tbsp coriander pesto (page 180)
175g (6oz) mashed potatoes

TO SERVE
200g (7oz) ready-prepared couscous
about 400ml (14fl oz) boiling
  vegetable stock (page 40)
handful of parsley leaves, chopped
drizzle of extra virgin olive oil
juice of 1 lemon

1 | Preheat the oven to 180°C/350°F/gas mark 4. Lightly cook the courgettes in boiling salted water for 5-10 minutes, or until tender. Refresh in cold water, pat dry, then rub with oil and sprinkle lightly with salt.

2 | Roast the aubergines and ceps for about 20 minutes. Top and tail the courgettes and cut them in half at an angle. Remove any seeds with an apple corer or paring knife, leaving a shell of about 5mm (¼in) thick. Leave the aubergines to drain, then halve them lengthways. Scoop out and reserve the flesh, leaving the skin and just enough flesh to hold it together. Blanch, skin and seed the tomatoes.

3 | For the green courgette stuffing, cook the lentils in boiling water for 30-40 minutes, or until tender. Heat the olive oil and sauté the shallots and garlic. Add the lentils and the rest of the ingredients. Mix, season, and use to stuff the green courgettes.

4 | For the yellow courgette stuffing, roughly chop the sun-dried tomatoes and combine with the cheeses. Season, then use to stuff the yellow courgettes.

5 | For the aubergine stuffing, heat the butter and sauté the spinach for 5 minutes. Mash in the goats' cheese, season and use to stuff the aubergines.

6 | For the cep stuffing, separate the stems of the roasted mushrooms from the caps. Using an apple corer, hollow out the stems and sauté the removed flesh in the butter with the herbs and breadcrumbs. Season and use to stuff the mushroom stems, then replace the caps.

7 | For the tomato stuffing, mash the coriander pesto into the dry mashed potato. Season and use to stuff the seeded tomatoes.

8 | Pour the couscous into a bowl, cover with boiling stock, then cover tightly with clingfilm. Leave to steam for 15 minutes, by which time the liquid should be fully absorbed. With a fork, fold in the chopped parsley with seasoning to taste, then pack into oiled moulds or ramekins and turn out in a neat mound on the serving plates.

9 | Arrange the stuffed vegetables around the couscous on a serving plate. Drizzle the couscous with the olive oil and lemon juice, and serve.

Courgette Flowers with Grilled Vegetables

Courgette flowers are a favourite at our restaurants in the summer, served as a starter on their own or as a main course with grilled vegetables.

SERVES 4

4 courgette flowers
vegetable oil for deep-frying
salt and black pepper
1 recipe quantity tempura batter
  (page 95)
1 recipe quantity sun-dried tomato
  and lentil salsa (page 187)

POLENTA
55g (2oz) butter, plus more for frying
50ml (2fl oz) double cream
good handful of thyme, oregano and
  rosemary, finely chopped

250g (9oz) quick-cook polenta
a little butter and olive oil, for frying

FILLING
1 large sweet potato, diced
a little olive oil
few sprigs of thyme, chopped
large knob of butter
1 banana shallot, or 2-3 ordinary
  shallots, finely chopped
1 garlic clove, finely chopped
dash of white wine
150g (5½oz) ricotta cheese

55g (2oz) Parmesan, freshly grated
nice handful of basil leaves, finely
  chopped, to finish
few drops of lemon juice
handful of pine nuts, toasted

GRILLED VEGETABLES
2 courgettes
1 large aubergine
a little sesame oil

1 | To make the filling, preheat the oven to 190°C/375°F/gas mark 5. Toss the sweet potato dice in the oil and thyme with some seasoning until well coated and tip on to a baking sheet. Roast for 12 minutes then leave to cool.

2 | Meanwhile, heat the butter and cook the shallot(s) and garlic gently until just softened. Add the white wine and cook until almost entirely reduced. Leave to cool.

3 | Prepare the vegetables. Cut the courgettes and aubergine lengthways into thin strips about 5cm (2in) long. Salt the aubergine and set aside for 30 minutes.

4 | For the polenta, bring 1 litre (1¾ pints) of water to the boil in a large pan with the butter, cream, herbs and seasoning to taste. Tip in the polenta and stir until well

mixed. Pour into a flat, lipped dish, rub a rolling pin with olive oil and roll it over the surface of the polenta to give a smooth finish, then allow to cool.

5 | In a large bowl, blend the cooled shallot and garlic mixture for the filling with the cheeses, then fold in the sweet potato, basil, lemon juice and pine nuts.

6 | Remove all the inner bits and pieces of the courgette flowers. Using a piping bag, fill each flower tightly with the filling, leaving space at the end to twist the petals together. Chill for 20 minutes.

7 | Towards the end of this time, turn the polenta out of the dish and cut it into 8cm (3¼in) squares, then halve these diagonally to form triangles. Fry these in a little butter and oil until crisp on both sides.

8 | To grill the vegetables, preheat the grill or griddle pan. Rinse the aubergine slices thoroughly and pat dry. Brush them and the courgette slices with sesame oil and grill or griddle for 2-3 minutes on each side, until softened and nicely coloured.

9 | In a wok, heat the oil for deep-frying until very hot and then dip the courgette flowers in the batter quickly, allowing excess batter to drip off, and fry in batches of two at a time until nicely coloured – 2-3 minutes. Drain briefly on kitchen paper.

10 | To serve, pile some salsa in the centre of each plate, arrange the polenta triangles and grilled vegetable slices around like the petals of a flower and place a stuffed courgette flower in the centre, on top of the salsa.

Asparagus and Potato Rotolo

The original Italian *rotolo* consists of pasta sheets rolled around a filling, usually ricotta cheese and spinach, which are then boiled and served with a sauce, normally tomato. We played with this idea using a mushroom stuffing, and eventually came up with this variation, and replaced the pasta with a sort of potato roulade.

SERVES 4
100ml (3½fl oz) double cream
salt and black pepper
6 medium-sized potatoes,
  cut thinly on a mandolin into
  slices about 1mm thick
  (the thinnest possible)
handful of thyme leaves,
  chopped

FILLING
1 bunch asparagus, trimmed
1 courgette, cut lengthwise into long
  thin slices
1 roasted red pepper
200g (7oz) ricotta cheese
2 tbsp basil pesto (page 178)
handful of grated Parmesan

TO SERVE
1 recipe quantity chilli coulis
  (page 182)
basil pesto (page 178)
balsamic reduction (page 198)

1 | Preheat the oven to 190°C/375°F/gas mark 5 and line a big square baking tray (about 35cm/14in) with baking paper. In a bowl, season the cream well and brush the paper lining lightly with it to prevent the potatoes sticking, then layer the potato slices overlapping in rows. Do another three layers, brushing each layer with the seasoned cream and sprinkling with a little thyme, finishing with a layer of cream. Cut out a piece of paper to fit over the potato and press it down well to compress everything into position.

2 | Bake the *rotolo* in the oven for 20-25 minutes, until the potatoes are tender, testing with the tip of knife. Leave to cool.

3 | For the filling, blanch the asparagus in boiling salted water for 1 minute and refresh in cold water. Griddle or lightly pan-fry the courgette slices until well coloured and softened. Skin the roasted pepper and cut it into long thick strips.

4 | To make the filling, cover a work surface with two layers of foil. Carefully transfer the potato assembly from the baking tray to the prepared work surface. Mix the ricotta, basil pesto and Parmesan, and spoon a thin band of that mixture about 2cm (¾in) wide along the near side of the sheet of potato. Arrange the asparagus on top of that, then behind that (i.e. away from you), arrange the courgette slices and the pepper strips on top of that.

5 | Using the foil, roll up the entire thing like a Swiss roll as tightly as possible, tucking the sides in as you go. Roll and wrap tightly in the foil, twist the ends to seal and chill for 1 hour.

6 | Preheat the oven to 200°C/400°F/gas mark 6. Using a very sharp knife, slice the roll across, still wrapped in foil, into four pieces. Line a baking tray with greaseproof paper, stand the four pieces of *rotolo* on their ends on it and bake for 10 minutes.

7 | Remove the foil, and serve the *rotolo* still standing on its end to show the inner layers, garnished with pools of the coulis, pesto and reduction.

Wild Mushroom Galette

You can make the potato flowers ahead of time: let them cool and store them wrapped and interleaved in sheets of greaseproof paper, and then warm them through in the oven when you want to serve them.

SERVES 4

55g (2oz) butter
500g (18oz) mixed wild mushrooms, such as ceps, chanterelles and trompettes, wiped clean
good handful of thyme leaves, chopped
salt and black pepper
olive oil
3 large oval potatoes, sliced on a mandolin to about 2mm/¹⁄₁₆in thick)

SALAD
125g (4½oz) each of rocket and baby spinach leaves
handful of herbs, such as basil and oregano
3 tbsp olive oil
1 tbsp lemon juice
handful of pine nuts, toasted

TO GARNISH (OPTIONAL)
4 little bundles each of carrot batons, green beans and asparagus tips
12 long sturdy chive stalks

1 | Heat the butter and sauté the mushrooms gently with some of the thyme and some seasoning until well cooked and soft.

2 | Using a 23cm (9in) frying pan, line it with a thin coating of oil and get it good and hot. Sprinkle one-quarter of the remaining thyme on the base of pan, then arrange one-quarter of the potato slices in it like the petals of a flower radiating outwards from the centre. Turn down the heat and cook gently for about 2 minutes until crisp on the underside. Season, turn over carefully using a fish slice, and cook for 2 minutes more. Remove from the pan and set aside to keep warm. Make three more potato galettes in the same way.

3 | Meanwhile, prepare the garnishes, if using. Blanch the little bundles of vegetables separately in boiling salted water until just tender, then refresh them in cold water and pat dry. Tie each bundle with a chive stalk.

4 | Make the salad by mixing the greens in a salad bowl. Make a dressing by whisking the oil and lemon juice together with seasoning to taste. Pour this over the salad, tip in the pine nuts and toss until everything is well coated.

5 | To serve, pile the salad in the centre of the serving plates, then arrange the sautéed mushrooms around the edge. Place a potato galette on top. If you like, garnish with the bundles of carrots, green beans and asparagus.

Wild Mushrooms

For the vegetarian cook, mushrooms are among the most versatile of foods and the most potent of flavourings. Since our early days, catering for music festivals in the countryside, we have celebrated this amazingly useful "food for free", and have both since become keen amateur mycologists.

We go foraging for mushrooms whenever we get the chance, whether it is in Epping Forest (or even Hyde Park) or further afield. Adrian even has his own secret spot in the Scottish Highlands that he disappears to in late summer to gather an abundance of chanterelles, ceps and hedgehogs, as well as slippery jacks, the local speciality. On one of those trips, he and his good friend Andressa found a *grifola frondosa* – or hen of the woods – the size of a football, and they still argue over who spotted it first.

We are among a relatively small band of enthusiasts in these islands, but at various times of the year in Continental Europe, especially in France and Italy, you will find cars and vans dotted all along woodland roads as people go scouring the earth for its tasty fruits. In both those countries, too, every pharmacist is required by law to be able to identify all the mushrooms that grow in their area so they can offer advice on what is or isn't safe to eat.

Nowadays, however, it is increasingly easy to buy "wild" mushrooms – guaranteed safe – at markets and in better supermarkets. As well as the most commonly seen oysters and shiitake, porcini (ceps), chanterelles, trompettes, enoki and puffballs are now quite easy to find in season. One of our favourites, *laetiporus sulphureus,* or chicken of the woods, is now even being cultivated, if still very expensively; as is the hen of the woods (or *maitake* in Japan) mentioned above, which is also being used

to treat cancer. Blewits, again regulars on our menus, are incredibly easy to find in the woods (and to identify), but is also the only European mushroom that can be cultivated on a commercial scale.

We try to stick to seasonality with our mushrooms, which is easier than you might first imagine, using St George's mushrooms in spring, chicken of the woods in the summer right through to the height of the true mushroom season in autumn. It is at this time that we have our regular fungi fests at the restaurants, each year trying to find new and even more interesting ways of presenting nature's bounty. Blewits start once the ceps and chanterelles have gone, but they grow on into January – and can even be picked frozen to defrost nicely in the kitchen.

Remember that you should, as much as possible, avoid washing most types of mushroom (except trompettes). Instead, brush them well or simply wipe them well with a slightly damp cloth.

Of course, dried versions of many types of mushrooms, notably ceps, chanterelles and morels, are available all year round, and can deliver almost as much flavour as the fresh fungus, although the texture is rubbery so it is best to chop them small. The liquid in which they are soaked also provides you with a useful stock.

Finally a big warning note. Never eat a wild mushroom that hasn't been properly identified by someone who really knows what they are doing. If you want to follow our example and go to pick your own, it is much the best idea to go on an organized fungi foray with an expert. We recommend Andy Overall of Fungitobewith (www.fungitobewith.org) – as well as being very knowledgeable, he is a lovely man.

Wild Mushroom Fricassee

There must be 1,001 ways of serving pan-fried mushrooms, but we think that in this dish everything works well together – and parts of it can be varied endlessly, according to availability, with almost equally good results. This is one of our favourite comfort dishes.

SERVES 4

450g (1lb) mixed wild mushrooms, e.g ceps, trompettes, chanterelles
55g (2oz) butter
2 tbsp olive oil
a few sprigs each of thyme and rosemary, chopped

SAUCE
55g (2oz) dried ceps
30g (1¼oz) butter
2 banana shallots, or 1 medium onion, finely chopped

1 small fennel bulb, roughly chopped
1 carrot, diced
1 celery stalk, chopped
a few sprigs each of thyme and rosemary
5 tbsp plain flour
150ml (5fl oz) Madeira

JERUSALEM ARTICHOKE MASH
600g (1lb 5oz) potatoes
salt and white pepper
600g (1lb 5oz) Jerusalem artichokes

a splash each of lemon juice and white wine vinegar
55g (2oz) butter, softened
25ml (1fl oz) double cream

BABY VEGETABLES
100g (3½oz) each of baby vegetables (carrots, sweetcorn, turnips, asparagus tips and fennel)
olive oil, to coat

1 | Preheat the oven to 190°C/375°F/gas mark 5. First make the sauce. Bring the ceps to the boil in 500ml (18fl oz) water then leave to soak for 20 minutes. Heat the butter and sweat the shallots, fennel, carrot, celery and herbs, then stir in the flour and cook briefly. Gradually (to avoid lumps) add the ceps, their soaking water and the Madeira. Bring to the boil, stirring, and simmer for about 30 minutes, then push through a sieve. Keep warm.

2 | Meanwhile, make the Jerusalem artichoke mash. Cook the potatoes in their skins in boiling salted water until just tender. Drain well. Peel the Jerusalem artichokes, cut into chunks and cook in boiling salted water (with a little lemon juice and white wine vinegar to keep their colour) until tender. Remove the skins from the potatoes and purée with the artichokes, adding the butter and cream and seasoning with salt and white pepper. Keep warm.

3 | Prepare the baby veg by scrubbing them all well, then blanching each separately for 2 minutes in salted boiling water, then refreshing them. Toss them all in olive oil and roast for 5 minutes.

4 | To cook the wild mushrooms, melt the butter and oil together in a large frying pan with the thyme and rosemary and cook the mushrooms until softened and tender. Stir into the hot sauce. Season to taste.

5 | To serve, using a pastry cutter, mould a mound of the mash in the middle of each serving plate, arrange the baby veg on top and spoon a pool of the mushrooms and sauce in front.

Saffron Tortellini

with Asparagus, Pine Nuts and Gorgonzola in a Sage and Herb Butter

The recipe for the sage and herb butter makes much more than you'll need here, but it is easier to make it in these quantities – you can use it later to dress all sorts of pasta and vegetable dishes.

SERVES 4

2 recipe quantities pasta dough (page 158, made with ½ tsp saffron strands in place of the thyme)
plain flour, for dusting
salt and black pepper
Parmesan shavings, to serve
12 roasted or grilled asparagus tips, to serve (optional)

FILLING
6 asparagus tips, thinly sliced across
100g (3½oz) Gorgonzola cheese, crumbled
2 tbsp pine nuts, toasted
handful of basil leaves, finely shredded

SAGE AND HERB BUTTER
250g (9oz) butter, softened
good handful of sage leaves, chopped
½ banana shallot, or 1-2 ordinary shallots, very finely chopped
few drops of lemon juice
finely grated zest of 1 lemon
pinch of finely chopped parsley

1 | A couple of hours ahead, prepare the filling. Blanch the asparagus for 1 minute in salted boiling water, refresh in cold water and drain. Pat dry and mix with the rest of the ingredients.

2 | On a well-floured surface, roll the pasta dough to a large rectangle and, using a 3cm (1¼in) pastry cutter, cut out 24 discs.

3 | Spoon some of the filling into the centre of one-half of each pasta round, fold over into a half moon, bring the two ends together like a napkin and pinch these together well to seal. Get the characteristic tortellini shape by then lightly folding over the centre of the curved top, opposite the join, back on itself. Allow to rest in a warm dry place for about 40 minutes, turn over and leave for the same time.

4 | To make the sage and herb butter, beat the butter until lighter in colour, then add all the other ingredients and combine well. Pop the mixture into the fridge briefly to firm it up slightly, then roll it into a cylinder inside a sheet of foil or clingfilm. Chill until nice and firm.

5 | Cook the tortellini in boiling salted water (in two batches) for about 2 minutes, until the pasta is *al dente*. Drain well.

6 | To serve, toss the cooked tortellini with four to five thick slices of the sage butter, then arrange on serving plates. Decorate with shaved Parmesan and garnish with asparagus tips as an optional extra.

Beetroot and Goat's Cheese Ravioli

For the beetroot juice, put a peeled raw beetroot through a juicer or grate a peeled raw beetroot and cover it in water for 2 hours. If you have ravioli moulds, they save lots of time and produce very good results.

SERVES 4
2 recipe quantities pasta dough (page 158, made without the thyme but adding about 50ml/2fl oz beetroot juice, see above)
plain flour, for dusting
1 egg, beaten
salt

FILLING
a little butter
4 banana shallots, or 6-8 ordinary shallots, halved and sliced
1 tbsp sugar
dash of white wine vinegar
200g (7oz) goat's cheese, crumbled
1 tbsp ricotta cheese

TO SERVE
rocket pesto (page 178)
shaved Parmesan cheese
olive tapenade (optional, page 202)

1 | A couple of hours ahead, prepare the filling. In the butter very gently cook the shallots with the sugar and white wine vinegar for about 10 minutes, stirring occasionally, until nicely caramelized. Set aside to cool. Mix the two cheeses in a bowl.

2 | On a well-floured surface, roll out the pasta dough to a 40 x 30cm (16 x 12in) rectangle, then divide this into 48 x 5cm (2in) pasta squares.

3 | Put a spoonful of the cheese mixture in the centre of each of half the squares and top that with some shallots. Moisten the edges of each square with beaten egg and place another pasta square on top. Pinch round the edges to seal well. Crimp round the edges with a fork to help the seal and to look decorative. Allow to rest in a warm dry place for about 40 minutes, turn over and leave for the same time.

4 | Cook the ravioli in boiling salted water (in two batches) for about 2 minutes each, until the pasta is *al dente*. Drain well.

5 | To serve, arrange the ravioli on serving plates, place a nice mound of rocket pesto in the middle, decorate with shaved Parmesan and dot olive tapenade around as an optional extra.

Butternut Squash Cannelloni

With the flavours and colours of the squash filling and the root vegetable and lentil salsa, this makes a wonderfully autumnal dish.

SERVES 4

PASTA DOUGH
100g (3½oz) plain flour, sifted
dash of olive oil
1 egg
a little chopped thyme
salt and black pepper

FILLING
1 small butternut squash, peeled, seeded and cubed
splash of olive oil

4 banana shallots, or 8 ordinary shallots, finely chopped
3-4 garlic cloves, finely chopped
500g (18oz) ricotta cheese
small handful of mixed basil, parsley and oregano, chopped

WATERCRESS SAUCE
splash of olive oil
1 banana shallot, or 2-3 ordinary shallots, finely chopped

1 garlic clove, finely chopped
dash of white wine
200ml (7fl oz) double cream
large bunch of watercress
few drops of lemon juice

TO SERVE
root vegetable and lentil salsa (page 186)
basil oil (page 194)
sun-dried tomato oil (page 194)

1 | To prepare the filling, preheat the oven to 190°C/375°F/gas mark 5. Toss the squash in a little of the olive oil until well coated and then roast for about 20 minutes, until tender. Allow to cool, then blend about two-thirds of it to a paste. Keep the oven on.

2 | Meanwhile, make the pasta dough. Mix all the ingredients together, with seasoning to taste, by hand. It may seem a very dry dough, but it will become more elastic as it is kneaded and rolled. Either rolling by hand or using a pasta machine, make the dough into 12 rectangles about 12 x 10cm (4½ x 4in).

3 | Heat a little oil in a heavy pan and sauté the shallots and garlic until just soft but not coloured. Transfer to a bowl and, once cool, mix in the squash, squash paste and the rest of the filling ingredients with seasoning to taste.

4 | Divide the filling between the pieces of pasta, arranging it in a line across their middles. Roll each piece up into a tube around the filling, trimming off most of the overlap and sealing the edges with a dab of water.

5 | Put the finished cannelloni in a deep baking tray and bake for about 10 minutes.

6 | Meanwhile, make the watercress sauce. Heat the oil in a heavy pan and gently sauté the shallots and garlic for a few minutes, until softened but not coloured. Add the wine and boil to reduce to almost nothing. Stir in the cream and bring to a bare simmer. Stir in the watercress and stir until nicely wilted. Purée the sauce, sieve and finish with a little lemon juice. Adjust the seasoning to taste, if necessary.

7 | Serve the cannelloni with the watercress sauce, some lentil salsa, basil oil and sun-dried tomato oil.

No-cook and other Fast Pasta Dishes

There are myriad sauces and dressings for pasta that can be ready in less time than it takes to cook dried or even fresh pasta. Even the cooking of the pasta can be speeded up: you know how long it seems to take to get a big pot of water boiling, so try heating half of the water in another pan or in a kettle. Nothing to do with speed, but a great tip from the lovely Ursula Ferrigno, who once cooked for us at the Hammersmith restaurant, is not to add salt to the water until it is actually at a good rolling boil. This way the salt does actually get mixed into the water; if added before, it can just end up coating the bottom and sides of the pan.

If you have a well-stocked store cupboard and some of our pestos and sauces from Chapter 5 in your fridge or freezer, then you are minutes away from a fast but flavourful pasta dish. Try these suggestions:
• Just stir into your pasta any of our pestos (with lots of grated Parmesan if you like) (pages 178-181), some salsa rossa (page 186), tomato salsa (page 184) or some sun-dried tomato and lentil salsa (page 187).
• Crush some roasted garlic (page 213) to a paste and stir in with some sun-dried tomato and lentil salsa (page 187).
• Toss in lots of chopped ripe plum tomatoes and our mascarpone sauce (page 191).
• Add a large jar of artichoke hearts, drained and roughly chopped, with a few spoonfuls of our olive tapenade (page 202).
• Crumble in some goat's cheese with a good sprinkling of our pickled lemon oil (page 194).
    If you have the time and/or inclination for the briefest spot of quick cooking, then you can:

• Dice any leftover veg, sauté lightly in a little olive oil, then stir into your pasta with a tsp of any of the pestos to bring it to life.
• Wilt some spinach in a little hot olive oil, stir in some sun-dried tomato and lentil salsa (page 187) and fork that through your pasta.
• Sauté some chopped shallots in hot olive oil, add some sliced mushrooms and cook gently for a minute or two, then add some halved cherry tomatoes, a small tub of double cream, some crumbled Gorgonzola and toss with the pasta.
• Simply sauté some mushrooms and add to the pasta with a little cep oil (page 194) or wild mushroom reduction (page 199).
    Always remember, when draining your pasta, to reserve some of the cooking water, as you can use this to thin any sauces or dressings down to the right consistency. Remember also that the pasta keeps on cooking as long as it is hot, and thus it will continue to absorb moisture from any dressing so it will continue to get thicker.

penne with sun-dried tomato pesto, green beans, mushrooms, parsley and pine nuts

Risotto alla Contadina

Wild garlic leaves make a wonderful springtime addition to this risotto. Shred the leaves and sauté with the vegetables. The garlic flowers, if you can get them, also make a lovely garnish.

SERVES 4

2 tbsp olive oil
75g (2¾oz) butter
2 leeks, well rinsed, trimmed (discarding dark green parts – use for stock) and finely chopped
500g (18oz) risotto rice
dash of white wine

about 1.5 litres (2¾ pints) simmering vegetable stock (page 40)
handful of wild garlic leaves with their flowers (optional)
3 asparagus stalks, cut at an angle into 2cm (¾in) lengths
30g (1¼oz) podded broad beans (in season)

½ courgette, cubed
1 tbsp each of chopped mint and parsley
salt and black pepper
55g (2oz) Parmesan, freshly grated, plus shavings to serve
2 tsp lemon juice

1 | Heat the oil and one-third of the butter in a deep heavy-based pan. Add the leeks and sauté until softened. Add the rice and stir until well coated in the fat. Increase the heat, add the wine and simmer gently. When most of the wine is absorbed, stir in a large ladleful of the hot stock. Cook over a moderate heat, stirring every few minutes and adding more stock as it is absorbed.

2 | After the rice has been cooking for about 15-20 minutes, heat half the remaining butter and sauté most of the wild garlic leaves, if using them, and the vegetables gently for 1-2 minutes.

3 | Stir the vegetables and their butter into the risotto with the next ladleful of stock. Stir in the herbs and seasoning to taste.

4 | Continue adding stock (or boiling water if that runs out) until the grains of rice taste creamy but still have some bite.

5 | Take off the heat and stir in the Parmesan and remaining butter, with more seasoning to taste if necessary and the lemon juice. Leave to sit for about 5 minutes, covered, before serving, garnished with some Parmesan shavings and the garlic flowers and some more whole leaves if you like.

Parsnip and Dolcelatte Risotto

We love parsnips and were looking for a way to bring out their sweet flavour. Their creaminess works really well in risotto.

SERVES 4

3 medium parsnips, cut into largish
  dice
2 tbsp olive oil, plus more for coating
  the parsnip
a little chopped thyme and rosemary
55g (2oz) butter

2-3 banana shallots, or 4-5 small
  ones, finely chopped
500g (18oz) risotto rice
dash of white wine
about 1.5 litres (2¾ pints) simmering
  vegetable stock (page 40)

salt and black pepper
100g (3½oz) Dolcelatte cheese, cut
  into cubes
2 tsp lemon juice
Parmesan shavings, to finish

1 | Preheat the oven to 180°C/350°F/gas mark 4. Toss the diced parsnips in a little oil with the herbs. Spread out on a baking tray and roast for about 30 minutes, until they are just beginning to give.

2 | Heat the oil and half the butter in a deep heavy-based pan. Add the shallots and sauté until softened. Add the rice and stir until well coated in the fat. Increase the heat, add the wine and simmer gently. When most of the wine has been absorbed, stir in a large ladleful of the hot stock. Cook over a moderate heat, stirring every few minutes and adding more stock as it is absorbed. Season to taste.

3 | Continue adding stock (or boiling water if that runs out) until the grains of rice taste creamy but still have some bite.

4 | Take off the heat and stir in the parsnips, Dolcelatte and remaining butter with more seasoning to taste if necessary and the lemon juice. Leave to sit for about 5 minutes, covered, before serving, scattered with the shaved Parmesan.

Ravia

An Italian chef who worked for us christened this *"ravia"*, which we assumed to mean "baby aubergines". We've since learned that in fact the name probably describes the presentation which, with its polenta "spokes", looks wheel-like, and *"ravia"* is a wheel for a *mille miglia* racing car.

SERVES 4
12 baby aubergines
a little olive oil
salt and black pepper
1 recipe quantity polenta triangles
  (page 144), to serve

SQUASH FILLING
½ butternut squash, peeled and diced
1 banana shallot, or 2-3 ordinary
  shallots, roughly chopped
1 garlic clove, finely chopped
a little olive oil

MUSHROOM FILLING
1 quantity mushroom duxelles (page 99)
150g (5½oz) ricotta cheese
75g (2¾oz) Parmesan, freshly grated
handful of chives, finely chopped

SPINACH AND CHEESE FILLING
250g (9oz) spinach leaves
55g (2oz) soft rindless goat's cheese
handful of basil leaves, finely chopped
handful of pine nuts
grated zest of 1 lemon

RATATOUILLE
drizzle of olive oil
1 small onion, finely chopped
1 red chilli, seeded and finely chopped
3 garlic cloves, finely chopped
1 x 200g can chopped tomatoes
1 small courgette, finely chopped
1 small aubergine, finely chopped
1 each of roasted red and yellow
  pepper, skinned, seeded and
  finely chopped
large handful of basil leaves, chopped

1 | To prepare the aubergines, preheat the oven to 190°C/375°F/gas mark 5. Cut off a slice from the rounded ends of the aubergines so they will sit upright with the stalk uppermost. Cut off the stalk end at the top, and then using a melon baller, scrape out the flesh from inside and discard, leaving a shell about 2mm (⅟₁₆in) thick. Toss these shells in oil, then roast for about 15 minutes, until they are beginning to wilt. Leave to cool. Increase the oven temperature to 200°C/400°F/gas mark 6.

2 | To make the squash filling, dice the squash, mix all the ingredients in a baking tray and roast for about 15 minutes. Remove from the oven and leave to cool. Reduce the oven temperature back to 190°C/375°F/gas mark 5.

3 | To make the mushroom filling, mix all the ingredients together and season to taste.

4 | To make the spinach and goats' cheese filling, remove the tough stems from the spinach and blanch it briefly in boiling water and refresh in cold water. Squeeze out as much of the water as you can. Fold the the remaining ingredients into the spinach and season to taste.

5 | To make the ratatouille, heat the olive oil in a pan and cook the onion, chilli and garlic for 4-5 minutes, until the onions are soft. Add the tomatoes and reduce to a thick sauce. Allow to cool to room temperature.

6 | While the ratatouille sauce is reducing. Heat a little oil and sauté the vegetables for the ratatouille until just tender – about 2 minutes for the courgettes and 5 minutes for the others. Allow to cool to room temperature.

7 | When ready to serve, line a baking sheet with greaseproof paper. Fill four of each of the aubergines with each stuffing. Place the stuffed aubergines, stalk end uppermost, on the baking sheet and cook for 10 minutes.

8 | To serve, stand the polenta triangles on their sides in the middle of each plate to make a 'Y'. Stir the ratatouille vegetables into the sauce with the basil and place a spoonful of the ratatouille in the centre, then place one of each type of stuffed aubergines between the polenta pieces.

Strudel

Here we tried to recreate some of the lovely flavour of the little lemony spinach pies you get in Syria and the Lebanon, called *sanbusak*.

SERVES 4

8 large sheets filo pastry
about 100g (3½oz) butter, melted
a handful of onion seeds
pasilla chilli and tomato jam
  (page 206), to serve

SPINACH AND OTHER FILLINGS

1kg (2¼lb) fresh spinach leaves,
  stalks removed
a little olive oil
3 banana shallots, or 6-8 ordinary
  shallots, finely chopped

2 large garlic cloves, finely chopped
juice of 1 lemon
small handful each of coriander and
  mint leaves, finely chopped
large handful of pine nuts, toasted
salt and black pepper
3-4 roasted red peppers, skinned
  and cut into flat rectangles
1 recipe quantity goat's cheese
  filling for ravioli (page 157)

GREEN OLIVE SAUCE

150g (5½oz) stoned green olives
15g (½oz) butter
1 banana shallot, or 2-3 ordinary
  shallots, finely chopped
2-3 garlic cloves, finely chopped
200ml (7fl oz) double cream

1 | For the green olive sauce, preheat the oven to 180°C/350°F/gas mark 4, put the olives in a baking tray and bake them for 2 hours until they begin to shrivel.

2 | To make the spinach filling, blanch the spinach briefly in boiling water, refresh in cold water, drain and squeeze out as much water as possible. Heat the oil and sweat the shallot and garlic gently until softened. Roughly chop the spinach and mix it into the shallots with the lemon juice, herbs, pine nuts and seasoning to taste.

3 | Turn the oven up to 220°C/425°F/gas mark 7. To assemble the strudel, arrange a sheet of the filo on a greased baking sheet and brush well with melted butter. Repeat with another sheet arranged on the first one so they half overlap. Spread the spinach filling over the half-overlapped and buttered sheets of filo. Arrange two more half-overlapped and buttered sheets of filo over that filling and spread with the roasted red peppers. Arrange two more half-overlapped and buttered sheets of filo over that filling and spread with the goat's cheese filling. Finish with the two remaining sheets of filo, half-overlapped and buttered as the base. Sprinkle the top with the onion seeds.

4 | Bake for about 12-15 minutes until the filo is golden.

5 | While the strudel bakes, finish the green olive sauce. Purée the olives in a food processor. Heat the butter and sweat the shallot and garlic gently until softened, add the olive purée and cook for 2-3 minutes. Stir in the cream.

6 | To serve, divide the strudel into four rectangular portions and then halve each portion diagonally and arrange the two pieces at an angle to each other on each plate. Pool the sauce around them and around that dot the chilli and tomato jam.

Schnitzel

Often, we also serve these with new potatoes roasted with rosemary and braised cabbage with caraway seeds.

SERVES 4
15g (½oz) butter
1 large leek, finely chopped
1 garlic clove, finely chopped
good splash of white wine
good splash of double cream
salt and black pepper
2 large tomatoes, blanched briefly and skinned
12 large long slices of aubergine, each about 2mm (⅛in) thick
basil pesto (page 178)
30g (1¼oz) Gruyère cheese, grated
seasoned flour, for dusting
1 egg, lightly beaten

55g (2oz) dry breadcrumbs
1 large plum tomato, for garnish
basil oil (optional, page 194), to garnish

HORSERADISH SAUCE
a little olive oil
knob of butter
2 banana shallots, finely chopped
1 celery stalk, finely chopped
1 carrot, finely chopped
about 75g (2¾oz) freshly grated horseradish

200ml (7fl oz) double cream
a few drops of lemon juice

GREENS
150g (5½oz) kale, tough stems removed and leaves roughly shredded
2 tbsp olive oil
few drops of lemon juice

1 | In a frying pan, heat the butter and sweat the leek and garlic over a gentle heat until soft. Add the white wine and reduce until almost all gone, then add the double cream and reduce that down too. Season to taste and set aside to cool.

2 | Cut each of the blanched tomatoes into four good slices. Spread four of the slices of aubergine with basil pesto to taste, then arrange two tomato slices on each of the pesto-spread aubergine slices. Put another layer of aubergine on top of that and spread that with the cooled leek mixture, covering it well. Sprinkle that generously with the cheese and finish with a final layer of aubergine slices.

3 | Dust each of the aubergine-layered schnitzels with flour, dip in egg and coat in breadcrumbs. Chill for 30 minutes, set on a tea-towel to take up moisture and keep the breadcrumbs dry.

4 | Preheat the oven to 220°C/425°F/gas mark 7. Transfer the schnitzels to a baking tray and bake for about 12 minutes, until nicely browned and the cheese is beginning to ooze out.

5 | While they cook, make the horseradish sauce. Heat the oil and butter together and sweat the shallots gently until softened. Add the celery and carrot and continue to sweat until tender. Stir in half the horseradish and add the cream. Bring to a simmer and add the rest of the horseradish, then bring back to a simmer for 1-2 minutes. Push through a sieve and finish with drops of lemon juice.

6 | At the same time, prepare the greens. Heat the olive oil in a frying pan and fry the kale until just wilted, then season and dress with the lemon juice.

7 | If you want a dash of colour on the plate, make a tomato concassé by quartering the tomato, scooping out the insides, patting the flesh dry with kitchen paper, then dicing. To serve, flood the plates with the sauce and put the greens in the middle by packing them into a pastry cutter. Halve the schnitzels at an angle and set two halves on top of each other on top of the greens. Dot more of the sauce around them and garnish with tomato concassé and herb oil if you have it.

Aubergine Charlotte

As many of the recipes in this part of the book will readily show you, we are constantly looking for new ways of using aubergine as a vehicle for flavours. This way soon established itself as a steady favourite.

SERVES 4
4 large aubergines
olive oil (optional)
8 oven-dried tomato halves
4-8 basil leaves

MUSHROOM STUFFING
15g (½oz) butter
2 tbsp olive oil
2 shallots, finely chopped
1 garlic clove, finely chopped
handful of herbs, ideally
  including basil, parsley and
  thyme, chopped
200g (7oz) mixed wild mushrooms
  (ideally including ceps), wiped
  and finely chopped

GOAT'S CHEESE CUSTARD
1 egg
250ml (9fl oz) double cream
200g (7oz) goat's cheese, plus more
  to finish

1 | Preheat the oven to 200°C/400°F/gas mark 6. From each aubergine, take a slice off the end opposite the stalk to remove the curve, then slice off a disc about 5mm (¼in) thick to act as the base for the charlotte. Then cut the aubergines lengthwise into slices about 5mm (¼in) thick.

2 | Chargrill the aubergine discs and slices or fry them briefly in a little oil until just tender. Allow to cool on kitchen paper.

3 | To make the mushroom stuffing, heat the butter and oil in a heavy-based pan and gently sweat the shallots with the garlic and herbs until the shallots are softened. Add the chopped mushrooms and cook for 4-5 minutes.

4 | To make the goat's cheese custard, beat the egg into the cream and bring slowly to a simmer. Immediately take off the heat, crumble in the cheese and mix in well.

5 | Line four charlotte moulds with foil, leaving lots of overhang. Then drop in the aubergine discs for the bases and line the sides with the slices, overlapping and again allowing the ends to overhang.

6 | Arrange the oven-dried tomatoes in the bottom of each aubergine, follow that with the mushroom stuffing, then the goats' cheese custard and top with the whole basil leaves. Finish with a slice or two of extra goat's cheese.

7 | Bring the overhanging slices of aubergine up and over to seal the top of the charlottes and bake them for about 15 minutes.

Aubergines
(Solanum Melongena)

The aubergine is the vegetarian cook's flexible friend, as it can be cooked in many ways and matches – as well as readily takes up – a wide range of added flavourings. This vegetable-fruit, a member of the tomato family, originated in Central Asia. It has been used throughout the Indian subcontinent and Arab world, where it is known as *brinjal*, for more than 1,500 years. As kids, we often enjoyed aubergines as baba ghanoush and in curries.

It is generally believed that the aubergine's arrival in Northern Europe is down to those Jews who fled the Spanish Inquisitors, and certainly fried aubergine has long been a common part of Jewish sabbath meals. Like the tomato, however, the aubergine was initially greeted with suspicion in Europe, and was thought to bring on insanity and called the "soothing mad apple", which gave it its Latin name.

Aubergines have also long been popular in Oriental cooking. Varieties in this part of the world, and in India, tend to be less club-like in shape and more spherical, as well as sometimes being pale in colour – hence their alternative name "eggplant", as they are known in the USA. Some are as small as grapes, but you have to be careful, as many of the Far Eastern varieties still tend to be very bitter.

Some Western cooks still salt their aubergines prior to cooking in order "to remove bitterness", but that has long been bred out of the varieties we can buy in Britain. Salting does, however, break down the cell structure of the flesh, which means that the aubergine will not absorb quite as much oil in the cooking process as it otherwise would.

We usually deal with this problem by grilling or baking aubergines. Nevertheless, before doing either we cut them into large chunks or thickish slices, salt them and squeeze out as much moisture as we can. The skin has all the flavour, hence in dishes such as aubergine caviar (page 192), where we are looking to bring out the vegetable's flavour, we use all the outside trimmings. Fortunately, dishes such as schnitzel (page 169), where the aubergine is more of a receptacle or sponge for other added flavourings, generally produce lots of useful ends and trimmings.

Nutritionally, aubergines are a bit of an oddity as they are not nearly as well endowed with the usual range of vitamins and minerals as most vegetable-fruits, but they do have considerable amounts of the bioflavonoids, phytochemicals that help renew arteries, prevent strokes and fight certain cancers. Always look for glossy unblemished skins and favour the slightly smaller specimens, as they will probably be younger and thus less tough and more sweet.

Pestos and all that Jazz

The recipes in this section are often used as garnishes to make dishes look exciting and to give flavour diversity. Alternatively, you can use them as side dishes and accompaniments – some even make good snacks, starters or party food.

Perhaps most importantly, though, keep a few of these dishes in your fridge and/or freezer and you will never be more than a few minutes away from having fabulously flavoursome dishes on your table. They can be used to lift and give zip to simple dishes such as a soup, a baked potato or a green salad, but many also make wonderful pasta sauces (see feature on page 160) or can be used as the basis of richly aromatic curries and noodle dishes.

Foods such as the pestos and, to a certain extent, the oils, provide a fail-safe means of preserving the freshness of herbs and other flavourings. So rather than letting what's left of that expensive bunch of basil wither away in a pot or in a plastic bag in the fridge, whiz up some pesto and you will be assured of enjoying every ounce of flavour the herb possesses.

Most of the things in this section benefit from being made ahead of time – anything from an hour or so to several weeks – to give the flavours a chance to amalgamate and develop. All will keep well in a sterilized container in the fridge, in an airtight jar or covered with a film of oil to keep the air out, where appropriate. Each recipe specifies how long it will keep in good condition.

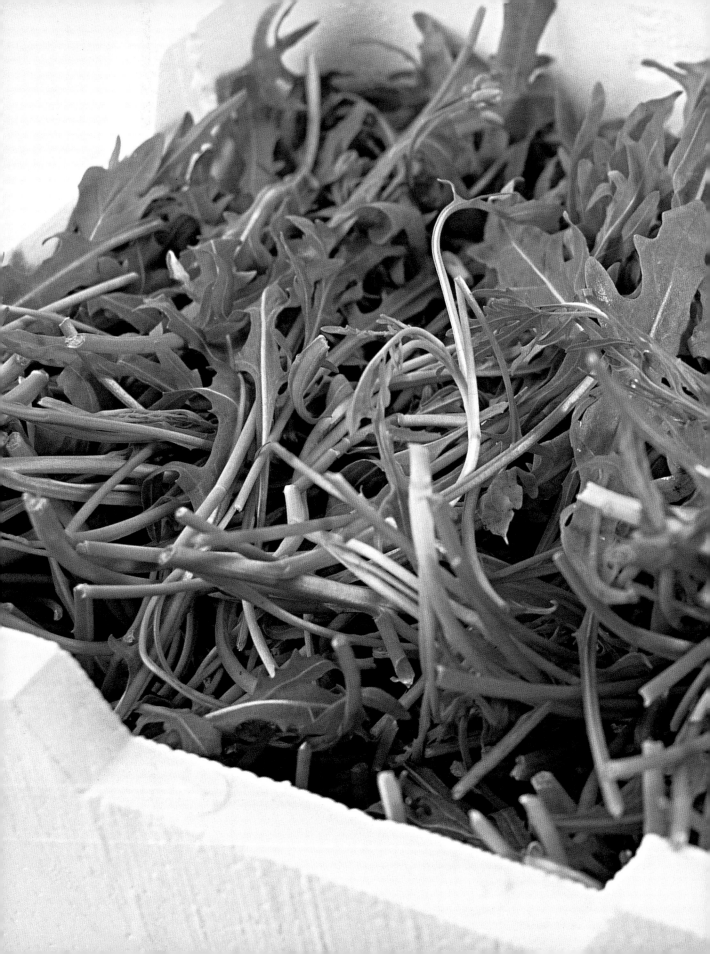

Basil Pesto

We don't add Parmesan to pestos. This way we keep vegans happy and the pestos can be used with a wider range of dishes. Of course, you can add grated Parmesan – a good handful should do it. When we add the nuts we keep them coarse.

MAKES ABOUT 225G (8OZ)
large bunch of basil leaves
juice of 1 lemon
1 fat garlic clove, finely chopped
200ml (7fl oz) extra virgin olive oil
55g (2oz) pine nuts, toasted
salt

1 | Using a mortar and pestle or food processor, blend the basil, lemon juice and garlic with the olive oil, starting with as little oil as possible to keep the herb's colour. Once you have a smoothish paste you can add the rest.

2 | Add the toasted pine nuts and blend briefly to a lumpy purée. Season with salt to taste. Store in the fridge for up to a month.

Rocket Pesto

This simple variation on basil pesto has an intriguing flavour. It is softer and more subtle than basil pesto, so goes with a wider range of ingredients. Sometimes we finish this with a few spoonfuls of cream for an even richer effect.

MAKES ABOUT 225G (8OZ)
large bunch of rocket leaves
juice of 1½ lemons
2 fat garlic cloves, finely chopped
200ml (7fl oz) extra virgin olive oil
55g (2oz) pine nuts, toasted
salt

1 | Using a mortar and pestle or food processor, blend the rocket, lemon juice and garlic with the olive oil, starting with as little oil as possible to keep the herb's colour. Note the greater amount of lemon juice and garlic to counter the rocket's pungency. Once you have a smoothish paste you can add the rest.

2 | Add the toasted pine nuts and blend briefly to a lumpy purée. Season with salt to taste. Store in the fridge for up to a week.

Coriander Pesto

The flavour of this pesto goes well with lots of Oriental-influenced dishes, as well as food in the Middle Eastern tradition such as the grilled haloumi on page 86, where it can take the place of the harissa.

MAKES ABOUT 225G (8OZ)
large bunch of coriander leaves
juice of 1 lemon
1 fat garlic clove, finely chopped
200ml (7fl oz) extra virgin olive oil
55g (2oz) pine nuts, toasted
salt

1 | Using a mortar and pestle or food processor, blend the coriander, lemon juice and garlic with the olive oil, starting with as little oil as possible to keep the herb's colour. Once you have a smoothish paste you can add the rest.

2 | Add the toasted pine nuts and blend briefly to a lumpy purée. Season with salt to taste. Store in the fridge for up to a month.

Sun-dried Tomato Pesto

The combination of almond and tomato works well. This pesto is great on canapés and can be used with grilled veg and to dress pasta, perhaps with chopped fresh chilli – when it's like a dry arrabbiata sauce.

MAKES 225G (8OZ)
125g (4½oz) sun-dried tomatoes
1 large garlic clove, roughly chopped
1 tsp balsamic vinegar
small handful of basil leaves, roughly torn
1 tsp caster sugar
150ml (5fl oz) extra virgin olive oil
100g (3½oz) shelled almonds, roasted and chopped
salt

1 | Using a mortar and pestle or food processor, blend the sun-dried tomatoes, garlic, vinegar, basil and sugar with the olive oil. Start with as little oil as possible to keep the herb's colour; once it is making a smoothish paste you can add the rest.

2 | Add the nuts and blend briefly to a lumpy purée. Season with salt to taste. Store in the fridge for up to a month.

Artichoke Pesto

More than just a sauce or dressing, this pesto is substantial enough to make a side dish in its own right.

MAKES 225G (8OZ)

100g (3½oz) shelled hazelnuts
150ml (5fl oz) extra virgin olive oil
2 banana shallots, or 5-6 ordinary shallots, chopped
1 garlic clove, finely chopped
pinch of rosemary leaves
2 artichokes, prepared and cooked as described
  on page 102, then pared down to the heart
  and diced
small handful of parsley
few drops of lemon juice

1 | Preheat the oven to 190°C/375°F/gas mark 5 and roast the hazelnuts on a baking tray for about 20 minutes, until nicely browned. Tip on to a damp tea-towel and rub in the towel to remove their skins. Crush coarsely.

2 | Heat a little of the oil in a frying pan and gently sweat the shallots with the garlic and rosemary until the shallots are softened. Add the diced artichoke and cook for 5-6 minutes on a moderate heat.

3 | Stir in the parsley, lemon juice and crushed nuts. Leave to cool. Store in the fridge for a week or so.

Chilli Coulis

Guaranteed to liven things up whenever it appears, this coulis is again useful for allowing people to adjust the strength of chilli to suit their taste. It can also be sweetened up by adding a higher proportion of sweet peppers to soften the flavour but still deliver the heat. Try replacing all (or all but one) of the chillies with sweet red peppers.

MAKES 150ML (5 FL OZ)
5 red chillies, roasted (page 193)
  and seeded
2 red peppers, roasted (page 193)
1 tsp caster sugar
100ml (3½fl oz) extra virgin olive oil
3-4 tsp white wine vinegar
2 tbsp *mirin* (Japanese sweet rice
  wine)

1 | Put the chillies, red peppers and caster sugar in a blender or food processor and blend together well.

2 | Add the oil, vinegar and *mirin*, and blend well again. Leave to stand for an hour, then pass through a sieve. Store in the fridge for up to a week.

Thai Red Curry Paste

For most dishes you will probably only need half the paste this recipe yields, but it is easier to make in this sort of quantity. It stores well (freeze it in ice-cube trays and then you can make quick little one- or two-portion curries whenever you feel like it), and you can use it for several dishes other than Thai curries, for example the Burmese kassa on page 130.

MAKES 125G (4OZ)

2 tbsp vegetable oil
2-3 shallots, finely chopped
7 lemongrass stalks, trimmed
about 15 lime leaves, stems removed
largish chunk of fresh root ginger,
 peeled

7 red chillies
largish chunk of galangal, peeled
1 garlic bulb, cloves separated

1 | Heat the oil in a frying pan and cook the shallots gently until softened. Add the remaining ingredients and cook for a few minutes, turning well.

2 | Blend the contents of the pan to a paste in a food processor.

Tomato Salsa

This fresh and pungent Mexican salsa is great with tortilla chips.

MAKES ABOUT 225G (8OZ)

4 tomatoes, skinned, seeded and chopped
1 red chilli, seeded and finely chopped
1 red pepper, roasted (page 193) skinned, seeded and
  finely diced
4 spring onions, finely chopped
good handful of coriander leaves, finely chopped
juice of 2 limes
4 tbsp extra virgin olive oil
salt

1 | Mix all the ingredients together with salt to taste. Store in the fridge for up to three days.

Pomegranate Salsa

This salsa is perfect whenever you need a fruity flavour. Adrian says of it: "Putting my fork into the pomegranate seeds makes me feel like a pirate opening up chests of glittering treasure and lifting it up and letting it run through your fingers, thinking how rich you are."

MAKES ABOUT 125G (4½OZ)

seeds from 1 pomegranate
2 spring onions, finely chopped
juice of 1 lime
handful of mint, finely chopped
3 tbsp extra virgin olive oil

1 | Mix all the ingredients together well. Store in the fridge for up to a week.

Salsa Rossa

A lovely fresh combination that looks as beautiful as it tastes, this salsa can be used with almost anything.

MAKES ABOUT 350G (12OZ)
100g (3½oz) sun-dried tomatoes, finely chopped
1 fat garlic clove, finely chopped (optional)
sprinkling of thyme and basil (optional)
2 each of roasted red and yellow peppers (page 193), skinned, seeded and finely chopped
1 large red onion, very finely chopped
2-3 tomatoes, blanched, skinned, seeded and diced
large handful of basil, shredded into strips
4-5 tbsp extra virgin olive oil, plus more to dress
pinch of sugar
dash of lemon juice
pinch of salt

1 | At least 3-4 hours before you want to use the salsa, mix together all the ingredients. If you are lucky enough to get sun-dried tomatoes bottled in oil with garlic and herbs, use them and some of their oil (in place of some of the extra virgin olive oil); otherwise add the garlic and fresh herbs.

2 | Put a few spoonfuls of the salsa in a food processor and pulse to a paste. Add this back to the salsa to bind the ingredients.

3 | Drizzle a little extra virgin olive oil over the top. Leave to sit for a few hours to let the flavours develop and ripen. Store in the fridge for up to a week.

Pineapple Salsa

The perfect foil for spicy dishes, this salsa is delightfully fresh and sweet and makes a great accompaniment to almost anything.

MAKES ABOUT 225G (8OZ)
¼ pineapple, peeled, cored and finely chopped
1 red chilli, seeded and finely chopped
grated zest of ½ lime
sprinkling of chopped mint and coriander

1 | Mix all the ingredients together and allow to sit for at least 30 minutes before using. Store in the fridge for up to four days.

Root Vegetable and Lentil Salsa

This salsa is substantial, warming and comforting.

MAKES ABOUT 225G (8OZ)
100g (3½oz) Puy lentils, soaked in cold water for 1 hour
2 carrots, 2 parsnips and 1 swede, finely diced, tossed in oil, chopped thyme and rosemary and seasoning
4-5 tbsp extra virgin olive oil
few drops of lemon juice
handful of basil leaves, chopped

1 | Preheat the oven to 230°C/450°F/ gas mark 8. Warm a roasting tray lined with greaseproof paper. Roast the vegetables for 10 minutes. Leave to cool. Drain the lentils and cover with cold water. Boil, then simmer for 10 minutes, until *al dente*. Drain and cool. Mix the oil, lemon and basil then season. Mix the lentils and vegetables with the dressing.

Pasilla Black Bean Salsa

This is an experiment with Mexican food. We wanted to use vegetables as stuffings instead of beans (e.g. in tortillas) and serve the beans in a fresher way as an accompaniment.

MAKES 250G (90Z)

150g (5½oz) dried black beans
2 dried pasilla chillies
1 fat garlic clove
1 red and 1 yellow pepper, roasted, skinned and
  seeded (page 193), then diced
3-4 spring onions, thinly sliced
1 red chilli, seeded and finely chopped
juice of 2 limes
4-5 tbsp extra virgin olive oil
good handful of coriander leaves, chopped

1 | Soak the beans in cold water for 2 hours. Bring to the boil in lots of fresh water, boil rapidly for 10 minutes and then simmer gently for about 35 minutes until just tender.

2 | Rehydrate the pasilla chillies in a small bowl of hot water for 30 minutes.

3 | Purée the rehydrated chillies and the garlic clove to a paste. Mix this paste into the drained beans together with the remaining ingredients. Store in the fridge for up to four days.

Sun-dried Tomato and Lentil Salsa

We're great fans of lentils, both for their nutritional value and their taste. This salsa is perfect in summer, especially as an accompaniment to a salad or pasta.

MAKES 350G (10½OZ)

150g (5½oz) Puy lentils
a little olive oil
1 banana shallot, or 2-3 ordinary shallots, finely chopped
1 garlic clove, finely chopped
dash of white wine
5 sun-dried tomatoes, finely chopped
1 roasted red pepper (page 193), seeded and chopped
3-4 spring onions, chopped
10-20 cherry tomatoes, halved
handful of basil leave, chopped

1 | Cook the lentils in boiling water for about 15-20 minutes, until just tender. Drain and set aside.

2 | Heat the oil in a large frying pan. Sweat the shallot(s) and garlic until just softened. Add the wine and boil it almost all off.

3 | Allow to cool and stir in the drained lentils and remaining ingredients. Store in the fridge for up to three days.

Aïoli

Thick, creamy and garlicky, this makes a wonderful accompaniment for any deep-fried dish, but can also be used as a salad dressing – try it with a new potato salad. The taste of this classic sauce of the south of France can be varied in lots of ways: by adding, say, lemon juice, chopped chilli, pickled lemon liquid, chopped herbs such as basil or rocket – even orange juice and segments for summer salads.

MAKES ABOUT 225G (8FL OZ)
3 egg yolks
1 tbsp French Dijon mustard
3 garlic cloves, finely chopped
50ml (2fl oz) olive oil
100ml (3½fl oz) light vegetable oil
100g (3½oz) yoghurt or crème fraîche
salt and black pepper

1 | Blend the egg yolks, mustard and garlic in a blender. With the machine running, slowly trickle in the olive oil, followed by the vegetable oil. When the sauce starts to emulsify and become creamy, you can add the oil more quickly.

2 | When all the oil is added, stir in the yoghurt or crème fraîche and season to taste. Store in the fridge for up to two weeks.

Mascarpone Sauce

This is our basic cream sauce, which is ideal for pasta. It is lovely as it is, but you can use it as a base for other flavours such as basil or watercress, whizzing in a handful of the leaves at the end.

MAKES ABOUT 350ML (12FL OZ)
a little oil
knob of butter
2 banana shallots, finely chopped
2 garlic cloves, finely chopped
1 celery stalk, finely chopped
1 carrot, finely chopped
splash of dry white wine
400ml (14fl oz) double cream
100g (3½oz) mascarpone cheese

1 | Heat the oil and butter together in a heavy-based pan and sweat the shallots, garlic, celery and carrot gently until softened.

2 | Add the wine and cook until it is almost evaporated.

3 | Stir in the cream and simmer for 5 minutes. Then add the cheese and stir until dissolved.

4 | Pass the mixture through a sieve. Store in the fridge for up to four days.

Aubergine Caviar

As this dish is best made from slices taken from the outside of the aubergine, with the skin on – it is a good way of using off-cuts from the *schnitzel* (page 169). It makes a good starter or snack on its own, as well as a fairly substantial accompaniment. As there are not too many highly flavoured additions, you get the full smoky taste of the roasted aubergine. The caviar is also good as a garnish for soups and salads, and is wonderful with grilled goat's cheese.

MAKES ABOUT 375G (13OZ)

about 300g (10½oz) outside aubergine flesh with skin (from 3-4 aubergines), diced fairly small
salt
4 tbsp olive oil

1 banana shallot, finely chopped
1 small garlic clove, finely chopped
1 tsp finely chopped chives
1 tbsp lemon juice
a little extra virgin olive oil

1 | Salt the diced aubergine and leave for about for 40-60 minutes. Rinse well, drain and squeeze out as much moisture as possible.

2 | Heat half the oil in a frying pan and fry the aubergine dice gently for a few minutes until softening. Heat the remaining oil in another pan and sweat the shallot and garlic gently until soft.

3 | Fold the shallot mixture into the aubergine with the chives and lemon juice. Leave to cool and dress with a little extra virgin olive oil.

4 | Store in the fridge for up to four days.

Red Schoog

Schoog is a Yemenite chilli sauce. It was a feature of our childhood holidays in Israel, part of the bustling excitement of the falafel stands in the bus station, which would offer an array of chilli sauces and salads with which to smother your falafel. In summer my grandmother would make a "green" Iraqi version of this dish, called *hil'ba*, for the Sabbath meal on Friday nights. It was made as here, but without tomatoes, and using green chillies and peppers, and packed with mint. Everyone would dollop a spoon of *hil'ba* on a plate and mop it up with warm *challah* (plaited bread).

MAKES 225G (80Z)
4 tbsp olive oil
5 red chillies
2-3 garlic cloves
2 red peppers

2 tomatoes, blanched and skinned
1 tsp ground fenugreek
a handful each of mint and
 coriander leaves

2-3 tbsp lemon pickling liquid
 (optional)
lemon juice
salt

1 | Preheat the oven to 190°C/375°F/gas mark 5. Pour the oil into a roasting pan and add the chillies, garlic, red peppers and tomatoes. Turn or shake them to coat them well in the oil and roast for 20 minutes, until the chillies are soft.

2 | Strain off the oil, skin the peppers and garlic and place the vegetables in a blender with the fenugreek. Blend until smooth, then pulse in the mint, coriander and strained oil, with the lemon pickling liquid if you have it, and a little lemon juice and salt to taste. Store in the fridge for up to a month.

Cep Oil

This makes a lovely dressing for salads or pasta, or drizzled into a creamy soup such as leek and potato.

MAKES ABOUT 300ML (10FL OZ)
300ml (10fl oz) light olive oil
55g (2oz) dried ceps
2 sprigs rosemary
2 garlic cloves, bruised

1 | In a pan, heat the olive oil. Add the ceps, rosemary and garlic and bring to a simmer. Simmer gently for about 15 minutes.

2 | Set aside in a cool place (not in the fridge) for two to three days, then pass through a sieve. Store in the fridge for up to a few months.

Pickled Lemon Oil

This simple preparation is great for salad dressings, drizzling on soups, giving an edge to sauces, etc.

MAKES 750ML (26FL OZ)
1 pickled lemon (page 113)
750ml (26fl oz) olive oil

1 | Put the pickled lemon in the olive oil and leave to soak for at least a couple of days in a cool place (not in the refrigerator).

2 | Store in the fridge for several months.

Basil Oil

As well as giving a wonderfully true basil flavour, the intense colour makes this a useful garnish.

MAKES 200ML (7FL OZ)
large bunch of basil leaves
few drops of lemon juice
1 fat garlic clove, finely chopped
200ml (7fl oz) extra virgin olive oil
salt

1 | Blend all the ingredients apart from the salt. Start with little oil; once you have a smoothish paste add the rest. Add salt to taste and leave overnight in a cool place (not the fridge). Pass through a sieve.

Sun-dried Tomato Oil

As a dressing, this is a useful "all-rounder" – with a good colour and a striking smoky tomato flavour.

MAKES ABOUT 225ML (8FL OZ)
125g (4½oz) sun-dried tomatoes
1 large garlic clove
small handful of basil leaves
1 tsp sugar
150ml (5fl oz) extra virgin olive oil
salt

1 | Blend all the ingredients apart from the salt. Start with little oil; once you have a smoothish paste add the rest. Add salt to taste and leave overnight in a cool place (not the fridge). Pass through a sieve.

Harissa

This version of the classic North African condiment spices up any dish, and allows you to moderate chilli hotness to individual taste.

MAKES 225G (8OZ)
6-7 red chillies, roasted (page 193),
  seeded and sliced
olive oil, to cover
2-3 red peppers, seeded and sliced
1 tbsp cumin seeds, toasted
2 tsp roasted garlic (page 213)
salt

1 | Put the chillies in a small pan, just cover with oil and cook slowly until very tender. Drain off the oil. Do the same with the red pepper slices.

2 | Pound together (or whiz in a blender) the cumin and roasted garlic with salt to taste. Mix in just enough of the combined drained-off oils to make a paste. Store in the fridge for up to a month.

Variation:
Ground toasted coriander and caraway seeds are also traditional ingredients added to harissa.

Balsamic Reduction

This makes a lovely garnish for all sorts of dishes and can be added to salad dressings as well as other sauces for depth of flavour - try adding a few drops to your next tomato sauce.

MAKES ABOUT 100ML (3½FL OZ)
150ml (5fl oz) good-quality balsamic
** vinegar**
1 spring onion, coarsely chopped
few sprigs each of thyme and
** rosemary, torn into pieces**
55g (2oz) caster sugar

1 | Mix all the ingredients in a smallish saucepan. Once the sugar has dissolved, bring to the boil and boil quite rapidly until reduced sufficiently to coat the back of a spoon (about half the original volume), but don't go too far and remember it will thicken even further when it cools.

2 | Store in the fridge for up to a month or two.

Wild Mushroom Reduction

The term "reduction" here is a bit of a misnomer, as the reduction achieved is so intensely flavoured it is rather like really dark chocolate, needing the butter and cream to moderate it and make it palatable. This very versatile sauce is a Gate fave and now a bit of a "classic". It obviously works well with wild mushrooms, but can be used in a wide range of dishes or added to other sauces for body.

MAKES ABOUT 750ML (26FL OZ)
55g (2oz) dried ceps
1.2 litres (2 pints) boiling water
knob of butter
a little vegetable oil
3 banana shallots, or 4-5 ordinary shallots, roughly chopped
1 garlic clove, chopped
2 sprigs rosemary (you can just use leftover stalks)
splash of wine
200g (7oz) butter, diced
500ml (18fl oz) double cream

1 | Soak the ceps in cold water for 5 minutes to get rid of dirt, then drain, rinse and put in a heatproof bowl. Cover with the boiling water and leave to stand for 30 minutes.

2 | Heat the butter and oil in a frying pan and sweat the shallots and garlic with the rosemary until the onion is just softened. Add the wine and boil it off. Add the rehydrated mushrooms and their stock, bring to the boil and simmer for 5 minutes. Pass through a sieve, squeezing to get as much liquid out as you can.

3 | Return this to the wiped-out pan and boil to reduce until it has quite a thick consistency. Be careful not to take it too far and scorch it.

4 | Dice the butter and whisk in until well mixed in, then mix in the double cream. Store in the fridge for up to three days.

Olive Tapenade

The deep, intense flavour of this preparation makes it a real palate bomb, but the good thing is that it still allows other flavours through.

MAKES 1KG (2¼LB)
1 kg (2 ¼lb) stoned black olives, well washed
1 red chilli, seeded and finely chopped
4 spring onions, finely chopped
3 garlic cloves, finely chopped
juice of 1 lemon
handful of basil leaves, finely chopped
extra virgin olive oil, for coating

1 | Roast the olives until shrivelled as described on page 168.

2 | Whiz them to a purée in a blender or food processor.

3 | Fold the remaining ingredients into the olive purée. Store in the fridge, coated with a film of extra virgin olive oil, for up to a month or two.

Seaweed Tapenade

A lovely accompaniment to nori and to many salads, this unusual tapenade can also be used to give an extra kick to miso soup and noodle dishes. The seaweed is almost too salty to be palatable, so we try to combine it with other things that reduce the saltiness. For the same reason, don't use salt-packed capers, but those bottled in vinegar.

MAKES ABOUT 275G (9½OZ)

200g (7oz) mixed seaweed, including *dulse*, *kelp* **and** *hijiki*, **rinsed under cold running water for 30 minutes**
1 banana shallot, finely chopped
small handful of coriander leaves, finely chopped
juice of 2 limes
small handful of capers, rinsed and chopped
drizzle of sesame oil
1 tbsp rice vinegar
1 tbsp *mirin* **(Japanese sweet rice wine)**
1 tbsp sesame seeds, toasted

1 | Drain the seaweed, squeeze out as much moisture as you can and chop finely.

2 | Mix with the remaining ingredients, finishing with a sprinkling of toasted sesame seeds. Store in the fridge for up to a month.

Coconut and Coriander Chutney

Sparklingly fresh with the bite of mint, lime and coriander, this goes particularly well with Oriental-style foods. It is also perfect with deep-fried food: we use it with the green banana fritters on page 66.

MAKES ABOUT 225G (8OZ)
1 small coconut, about 150g (5½oz)
knob of fresh root ginger, cut into
 julienne strips
a little vegetable oil
handful each of coriander and mint
 leaves, shredded
1 small red chilli, seeded and finely
 chopped
drizzle of sesame oil
juice of 2 limes and grated zest of 1
1 tbsp black mustard seeds, toasted
salt

1 | Using a potato peeler, peel off the dark skin from the coconut and soak the coconut for an hour in cold water, then shred it on a fine grater.

2 | Heat the vegetable oil. Fry the ginger for 30 seconds, then mix with the shredded coconut and the remaining ingredients and season with salt to taste. Store in the fridge for up to 3-4 days.

Green Mango Chutney

When you taste this you'll be convinced that it contains lime juice, but no lime is included – it is just the natural tart flavour of the green mango. You can get green mangoes in Asian food stores and ethnic markets. The chutney is good with all types of Oriental-influenced dishes and makes a lovely fresh moist dip to serve with fritters of all types.

MAKES ABOUT 150G (5½OZ)

1 green mango, peeled and grated
very large knob of fresh root ginger,
  peeled and grated
large bunch of coriander leaves,
  roughly chopped
1 green chilli, seeded and roughly
  chopped
salt
touch of extra virgin olive oil

1 | Put all the ingredients in a blender and purée until they make a smoothish paste. You may have to add a little splash of water.

2 | Store in the fridge for up to a week.

Pasilla Chilli and Tomato Jam

This is good with anything that needs a sharp pungent dressing – and it is fantastic with cheese.

MAKES ABOUT 225G (8OZ)

2 pasilla chillies
3 tbsp olive oil
2 red onions, halved through the root and then cut into slices
1 fresh red chilli, seeded and finely chopped
6 large tomatoes, blanched, skinned, seeded and diced
4-5 sun-dried tomatoes, roughly chopped
a good splash of white wine vinegar
4 tbsp light muscovado sugar

1 | Soak the pasilla chillies in hot water just to cover in a warm place for about 1 hour.

2 | Drain the chillies, reserving the soaking water, seed and roughly chop. Purée with 5 tbsp of the reserved soaking water.

3 | Heat the oil in a frying pan and sweat the onions and fresh chilli until just softening, then add the tomatoes, sun-dried tomatoes, pasilla mixture, vinegar and sugar. Cover and cook for about 45 minutes, until the tomatoes and onions are broken down and the mix has a nice jammy texture (remove the pan lid after 30 minutes to help it to dry out).

4 | Store in the fridge for up to a month.

Guacamole

If you are lucky enough to get avocados at that really perfect point of ripeness, dice them and make this into a salsa. Otherwise, purée them in a blender or mash them with a fork. Try to find Hass avocados as they seem to ripen more naturally, and deliver a much better flavour and creamy texture. The Mexicans call avocados "cream of the trees", and Hass can be exactly that.

MAKES ABOUT 225G (8OZ)

2 avocados
1 tomato, seeded and diced
handful of coriander leaves, finely chopped
juice of 1 lime
1 small red chilli, seeded and finely chopped
drizzle of extra virgin olive oil
5 spring onions, finely chopped
salt and black pepper

1 | Peel, stone and roughly chop the avocados, then mix with the remaining ingredients.

2 | Store in the fridge for up to two days.

Couscous

This is our basic couscous recipe, which we adapt in many ways to suit different dishes.

MAKES ABOUT 500G (18OZ)

350g (12oz) couscous
a little extra virgin olive oil, plus more for greasing
salt and black pepper
700ml (1¼pints) boiling water or stock
3-4 banana shallots, or 5-6 ordinary shallots, halved and sliced into crescents

100g (3½oz) shelled pistachio nuts
bunch of spring onions, thinly sliced
small handful each of coriander and parsley leaves, chopped

1 | Put the couscous in a bowl and mix well with 2 tbsp of the olive oil and a tsp of salt. Pour over the boiling water and cover with cling film. Leave in a warm place for 1 hour.

2 | Towards the end of this time, heat the remaining olive oil and sauté the shallots until very soft. Add to the couscous and mix well. Toast the pistachios in a dry pan, then grind into large chunks.

3 | Just before serving, add the pistachios and the rest of the ingredients to the couscous, season to taste and mix well. Store in the fridge for up to four days.

Gate Bread

The Gate bread has long been a favourite with our customers.

MAKES 1 LARGE LOAF
20g (¾oz) active dry yeast
4 tsp sugar
500ml (18fl oz) warm water
1kg (2¼lb) plain flour
salt and black pepper

bunch each of thyme and rosemary,
**   most coarsely chopped**
175ml (6fl oz) extra virgin olive oil
about 1½ tbsp sun-dried tomato
**   pesto (page 180)**

handful of cherry tomatoes, halved,
**   or plum tomatoes, sliced**
1 red onion, sliced or cut into thin
**   wedges**

1 | In a small bowl, mix the yeast with the sugar and warm water. Leave for 10-15 minutes until frothy.

2 | Stir this into one-third of the flour. Mix up 4tsp of combined salt, chopped herbs and black pepper into the remaining flour. Combine the two flour mixes together with the olive oil and pesto, then knead vigorously for 10-15 minutes using the heel of the hand.

3 | Shape into a long flattish loaf, drizzle with a little more oil, sprinkle with the remaining herbs in small sprigs, the sliced tomato and red onion wedges. Season the top and leave in a draught-free place for 40 minutes to prove.

4 | Preheat the oven to 180°C/350°F/gas mark 4 and bake for 40-45 minutes, until nicely coloured and the base sounds hollow when tapped.

5 | Leave for at least 15 minutes before slicing.

Roasted Garlic

Just as the pestos are a wonderful way of preserving fresh herbs, this is an excellent way of keeping garlic in a form that allows it to be added to lots of dishes without any further cooking. So next time you find that you've accumulated six garlic bulbs from buying one every time you shop, roast them as follows.

several garlic bulbs
olive oil for drizzling

1 | Preheat the oven to 180°C/350°F/gas mark 4 (it's usually best to make this when you are cooking something else in the oven at this temperature). If there are too many outside layers of skin on the garlic bulbs, pull them off first. Drizzle the bulbs with olive oil until it goes right inside and roast for about 60 minutes, until soft and squishy. Cut off the top of the heads with a serrated knife and squeeze out the garlic pulp.

2 | Use in soups, sauces, pestos and as a simple dressing on its own. The roasted garlic will keep in the fridge for up to a month. Make sure you keep it in a tightly sealed container.

Puddings

Sad to say, vegetarian restaurants are often associated with stodgy, heavy desserts that can seem like an apology for the fact that the cook thinks he hasn't fed you properly! We try to provide a range of puds to suit different appetites, occasions and seasons.

We like desserts to be light and just sweet enough to switch off the appetite. The Indo-Arabic attitude towards sweet dishes is that they should freshen the palate and please the eye. We play with flavourings in puddings as much as we do in our savoury dishes, sometimes adding a little spice. Our passion for perfumed flavours such as orange blossom and rose waters, cardamom, lemongrass, lavender and elderflower, comes to the fore here too, especially when cooking with fruit.

We employ the same philosophy for less popular fruits, such as quince, as we do for undervalued vegetables, showcasing them in dishes that highlight their taste and texture. We hope this will encourage people to cook them at home!

Above all, we never forget that, no matter how good and memorable the previous courses have been, the dessert usually leaves the most lasting impression, so it not only has to live up to what has gone before it – it has to be that little bit better.

Quince and Cardamom Almond Tart

This tart was inspired by the idea of adding fruit to baklava (page 225). Apples were traditionally cooked with these flavourings as part of the feast to celebrate the Jewish New Year, but quince tastes even better! In fact we suspect that quince was originally used and that apples later took their place.

SERVES 6-8

3 large quinces, peeled, cored and halved
400g (14oz) unsalted butter
450g (1lb) caster sugar
grated zest of 2 oranges
300g (10½oz) plain flour
400g (14oz) ground almonds
seeds from 6 cardamom pods, crushed

6 eggs, beaten
1 x 25cm (10in) sweet shortcrust pastry case, baked blind (page 231)

CARDAMOM SUGAR SYRUP
seeds from 4 cardamom pods, crushed
4 cloves
75g (2 ¾oz) caster sugar

ORANGE BLOSSOM SYRUP
300g (10½oz) caster sugar
2 tbsp orange blossom water

1 | To make the cardamom sugar syrup, put the cardamom seeds, cloves and sugar in a small pan with 300ml (10fl oz) water. Bring to the boil, stirring to dissolve the sugar, and simmer for another couple of minutes.

2 | Add the quince halves and poach gently for 25-40 minutes, depending on the variety and how ripe they are, until just tender. With a slotted spoon, remove from the syrup and allow to cool.

3 | While the quince halves are cooling, preheat the oven to 180°C/350°F/gas mark 4. Cream the butter and sugar together with the orange zest until pale. Mix the flour, almonds and cardamom seeds together, then fold alternating spoonfuls of that and the eggs into the creamed butter mixture.

4 | Spoon this mixture into the pastry case and arrange the cooled quince halves on top. Bake for 40 minutes, until the filling is just set.

5 | While the tart is cooking, boil the cardamom syrup to reduce it by half.

6 | At the same time, make the orange blossom syrup. Put the sugar and orange blossom water in a pan with 300ml (10fl oz) water, bring to the boil and simmer, stirring from time to time, for about 10 minutes, brushing the edges of the pan with water from time to time to stop the syrup burning at the sides.

7 | Remove the cooked tart from the oven, brush the quince with the reduced cardamom syrup, and leave to cool.

8 | Serve the tart cut into wedges, drizzled with the warm orange blossom syrup.

Quince

(Cydonia oblonga, Cydonia cydonia)

This wonderfully aromatic fruit from a central Asian tree of the rose family resembles a hard-fleshed yellow apple. Nowadays it tends to be ignored, probably because it is usually a bit acidic and dry if eaten raw, and normally requires lengthy cooking and sweetening.

The quince does, however, carry a long and noble history. It has been cultivated for more than 4,000 years and was among the most prized fruits in Ancient Greece and Rome, where it was regarded as sacred to Aphrodite/Venus, goddess of love. The quince was also thought to be the forbidden fruit of the Garden of Eden. Later, it became the first fruit to be used to make marmalade, which got its name from the Portuguese term for quince, "marmelo".

Cooked with other fruit, quince develops and enhances their flavours, and in Medieval England it was often added to apple pies or stuffed and baked like apples. It has long been a mainstay of Middle Eastern cooking, particularly that of Persia, where it was used a lot in meat and poultry dishes, and much valued for the way it combined with and set off spices.

Perhaps the most enduring use of the quince has been in preserves, as jams and jellies, and in butter and paste form. In France they call quince paste "cotignac" and it is sold as a sweet, while in Italy it is called "cotognata" and can be rendered savoury with added mustard seeds for serving with meat and chicken. In Spain, Portugal and South American their membrillo often accompanies cheese.

At the Gate, we normally bake quince rather than using the more common techniques of poaching and stewing it and, as you might expect, we try to make the best use of its affinity with spices. It is unlikely you'll find any quinces in supermarkets but, unless you are lucky enough to know someone who has a tree (and there are an amazing number languishing unharvested in large established gardens), go to ethnic street markets or Middle Eastern grocers and the chances are you'll find them there from about late October until around February. Look for nice big smooth specimens (as these have less wastage) that have little or no signs of green on the skin, and handle them carefully as, even though they stay rock hard, they do bruise incredibly easily. They will keep in the fridge for up to two months.

Poached Quince with Winter Fruits

Cooking times for quinces vary enormously through the year, so you really have to keep an eye on them, as they can take a long time or surprise you by how quickly they cook. In the restaurants, this dish is normally served with honey and ginger ice cream.

SERVES 4
2 medium quinces
crème fraîche, to serve

POACHING LIQUID
175ml (6fl oz) each of Marsala and a robust fruity red wine
2 star anise
1 cinnamon stick

2 lime leaves
juice of 3 oranges and 2 limes
big chunk of fresh root ginger
1 lemongrass stalk, split down the middle
75g (2¾oz) each of runny honey and caster sugar

WINTER FRUITS
75g (2¾oz) each of dried apricots, dried figs and dried apples

1 | Put all the ingredients for the poaching liquid in a large saucepan and bring to a simmer, stirring from time to time.

2 | Meanwhile, peel, core and quarter the quinces, then add them to the simmering poaching liquid, cover and continue to simmer for 20-30 minutes, until tender (see the introduction).

3 | When the quinces are almost ready, stir in the winter fruits and simmer for 5 minutes more.

4 | Serve in shallows bowls, dressed with crème fraîche.

Lemon Polenta Cake with Poached Pear

Adrian developed this recipe from a dessert he'd had on a trip to Brazil, using polenta rather than maize meal. It makes a nice light pud and is great served with coffee.

SERVES 6-8

4 large ripe pears, peeled, halved
  and cored
425g (15oz) butter, plus more for
  greasing
plain flour, for dusting
450g (1lb) caster sugar

grated zest of 5 lemons
450g (450g) pine nuts
200g (7oz) fine polenta
2 tsp baking powder
5 eggs, lightly beaten
mascarpone cheese, to serve

VANILLA SUGAR SYRUP
75g (2¾oz) caster sugar
1 vanilla pod, split and the seeds
  scraped out

1 | To make the vanilla sugar syrup, put the sugar in a small pan with 300ml (10fl oz) water and the vanilla pod and seeds. Bring to the boil, stirring to dissolve the sugar, and simmer for another couple of minutes.

2 | Add the pears and poach gently for anything from 5-25 minutes, depending on the variety of pear and how ripe they are, until just tender. With a slotted spoon, remove from the syrup and allow to cool.

3 | Preheat the oven to 180°C/350°F/gas mark 4, and butter a 23cm (9in) cake tin, then dust it with flour. Cream the butter and sugar with the lemon zest until pale. Whiz half the pine nuts to fine crumbs in a blender or food processor. Mix the whole and ground pine nuts with the polenta and baking powder. Add this and the eggs to the creamed butter mixture in alternating spoonfuls.

4 | Arrange the pear halves around the bottom of the prepared tin, pour the polenta mixture on top and bake for about 1 hour. Leave to cool in the tin.

5 | Serve cut in wedges, with a dollop of mascarpone.

Raspberry Brûlée

We have tried lots of versions of the classic brûlée over the years, but we think that this combination – the sharp flavour and yielding texture of the fruit against the soft sweetness of the custard and the crispness of the topping – is unbeatable.

SERVES 4
60g (2¼oz) caster sugar
300ml (10fl oz) double cream
½ vanilla pod, split and seeds
  scraped out and reserved
3 egg yolks
about 20 raspberries

TOPPING
about 2 level tbsp each of caster
  sugar and brown demerara sugar

1 | Preheat the oven to 180°C/350°F/gas mark 4. In a saucepan, mix half the sugar and all the cream with the vanilla pod and bring to a simmer.

2 | In a large mixing bowl, beat together the remaining sugar and the egg yolks with the vanilla seeds, then slowly whisk the hot cream mixture into the egg mixture. Return to the pan and bring just to a simmer.

3 | Meanwhile, arrange the berries in the bottom of four 6cm (2½in) ramekins.

4 | Sieve the custard into a measuring jug, leave to rest for 10 minutes, then pour into the ramekin dishes.

5 | Arrange the ramekins in a bain-marie (or a deep roasting tray half-filled with hot water) and place in the oven for about 25 minutes, until the custard is just set, but still with a bit of wobble when moved. Allow to cool.

6 | To make the topping, sprinkle the mixed sugars on top and, ideally using a blowtorch or, if not, under a very hot grill, cook the topping until the sugar has melted. Leave to cool again before serving.

Lavender and Pistachio Brûlées

After tasting a pistachio brûlèe in a restaurant, Adrian liked the idea but wanted to experiment with the flavours, so he tried adding the floral note of the lavender.

SERVES 4

about 100g (3½oz) shelled pistachios
60g (2¼oz) caster sugar
300ml (10fl oz) double cream
1 tbsp chopped lavender flowers (fresh or dried)
3 egg yolks

TOPPING
about 2 level tbsp each of caster sugar and brown demerara sugar

1 | Lightly toast the pistachios and pound all but 10g of them to a paste using a pestle and mortar.

2 | Mix half the sugar and all the cream with the pistachio paste and lavender in a saucepan and bring to a simmer. Set aside for at least 2 hours to allow the flavours to infuse.

3 | Preheat the oven to 180°C/350°F/gas mark 4. Reheat the cream mixture gently. In a large mixing bowl, beat together the remaining sugar and the egg yolks, then slowly whisk the cream mix into the egg mix, return to the pan and bring just to a simmer. Sieve into a measuring jug, pressing down well with the back of a spoon, or ladle to get as much flavour out of the nuts and flowers as you can, and leave to rest for 10 minutes.

4 | Pour into four 6cm (2/in) ramekins and put these in a bain-marie (or a deep roasting tray half-filled with hot water) in the oven for about 25 minutes, until just set but still with a bit of wobble when moved. Allow to cool.

5 | To make the topping, sprinkle the mixed sugars on top and, ideally using a blowtorch or, if not, under a very hot grill, cook the topping until the sugar has melted. Leave to cool again.

6 | Chop the remaining nuts and sprinkle over the top of each brûlée to serve.

Fruit Coulis

You can make this sort of coulis with any soft summer fruit. To give it an extra kick, you can add a splash of an appropriate fruit brandy if you like.

MAKES 125ML (4FL OZ)
150g (5½oz) soft summer fruit of
  choice, any stems, stalks etc
  removed
icing sugar, to taste

1 | Put the fruit in a pan, barely cover with water and bring to the boil. Simmer, stirring, for a minute or two until the fruit breaks down slightly.

2 | Push through a sieve and sweeten, if necessary, with icing sugar. Serve hot or cold.

Crème Anglaise

This classic is used in various ways for lots of our desserts. You can use the left-over egg whites for making pavlova (page 246) or some other meringue. It's easy to make variations of *crème anglaise*, say by adding stem ginger puréed with its syrup or infusing it with alcohol.

MAKES 600ML (1 PINT)
100g (3½oz) caster sugar
250ml (9fl oz) double cream
250ml (9fl oz) whole milk
½ vanilla pod, seeds scraped out
5 egg yolks

1 | Mix half the sugar, all the cream and all the milk with the vanilla pod and seeds in a pan and bring to just below the boil. Bring a little water to a simmer in a pan in which a big mixing bowl, preferably metal, will sit stably.

2 | In the large mixing bowl, beat together the remaining sugar and the egg yolks, then slowly whisk in the cream mix. Set the bowl over the pan of simmering water (not touching the water) and cook very gently, stirring constantly, for 10 minutes, until thick enough to coat the back of a spoon. Take off the heat and stir frequently for the first minute or two.

3 | Sieve into a bowl or jug. If you want to let it cool, cover the surface with greaseproof paper or clingfilm to avoid a skin forming.

Hungarian Apple Pie

George, the enigmatic Hungarian 'strudel king' who taught Adrian to bake in the Viennese style, gave him this recipe. The flavour of the pastry works beautifully with the apple filling. You need to chop the apples quite small as they aren't cooked before they go into the tart. If you have any pastry left over, mix in some chopped almonds, walnuts or pistachios and make into biscuits to cook alongside the tart for about 10 minutes, until golden.

SERVES 10-12
for the pastry
650g (1lb 7oz) plain flour
good pinch of ground cinnamon
pinch of baking powder
275g (9 1/2oz) caster sugar
175g (6oz) chilled butter, diced
2 eggs, lightly beaten, plus 1 more for glazing

1 tbsp soured cream
grated zest and juice of 1 lemon
pinch of salt

FOR THE FILLING
1.25kg (2 3/4lb) Granny Smith apples, peeled, cored and cut into 5mm(1/4in) dice

grated zest of 2 lemons
280g (10oz) caster sugar
good pinch of ground cinnamon
75g (2 3/4oz) sponge fingers, grated or whizzed into crumbs

TO SERVE
whipped cream

1 | To make the pastry, sift the flour into a large mixing bowl and add the cinnamon, baking powder, sugar and salt. Rub in the butter until the mixture has the texture of coarse breadcrumbs. Then make a hollow in the centre and add the beaten eggs, soured cream, lemon zest and juice. Using your hand or a fork, mix well and bring everything together into a soft ball of dough. Allow to rest in the refrigerator for 30 minutes.

2 | Preheat the oven to 180°C/350°F/gas mark 4, and line the base of a 25cm (10in) springform cake tin with greaseproof paper. Roll out about one-third of the dough slightly thicker than the normal pie thickness and use to line the bottom of the tin. Score with a fork or knife to prevent it puffing up and bake blind for about 10-15 minutes until quite well cooked. Leave to cool.

3 | Make the filling by mixing together everything except one-third of the biscuits.

4 | Using most of the trimmings from lining the cake tin bottom, roll out a long strip of the pastry and use to line the sides of the cake tin with a bit of an overhang. First mould into a long sausage with your hands and then roll it flat - you could even press it into place with your finger as this pastry is so malleable.

5 | Scatter the remaining crumbled biscuits over the base. Strain the apples in a fine sieve to get rid of as much liquid as possible and pile them into the tin. Press down and level the top with the back of a spoon, especially around the edges, otherwise they will collapse in. Fold in the overhanging pastry. Roll the remaining pastry and use to make a top. Lift into place

rolled around the rolling pin and then secure by pressing down. Give a very light egg wash to glaze and score a few holes in the top to let the steam out.

6 | Bake for about 1 hour, until well browned and incredibly aromatic. After about 45 minutes of this time, check and, if it is browning too rapidly, either reduce the heat slightly or cover the top with foil.

7 | Remove from the oven, allow to cool, and turn out (this should be quite easy as the pastry will have shrunk away slightly all round from the tin). Serve with whipped cream.

Amaretto Tart

This is a particularly quick and easy summer dessert, especially if you make the bases three to four days ahead and then fill and top them at the last moment.

SERVES 4

BASES
400g (14oz) amaretti biscuits, crushed
grated zest of 2 oranges
about 75g (2¾oz) skinned hazelnuts, coarsely chopped
1 tsp ground cinnamon
about 75g (2¾oz) butter, melted

FILLING
150g (5½oz) mascarpone cheese
seeds from 1 vanilla pod
dash of amaretto liqueur
5 tbsp double cream

TOPPING
250g (9oz) mixed summer fruit and berries
sprigs of mint, to decorate

1 | To make the bases, mix all the ingredients together and press one-quarter into an 8cm (3¼in) pastry cutter, bringing it up around the edge inside the cutter to form a concave centre. Chill briefly until the base comes out of the cutter easily, then make three more in the same way.

2 | To make the filling, whip all the ingredients together until semi-whipped but still loose. Spoon into the concavities of the bases, and top each with a cluster of the mixed summer fruit and berries. Decorate with mint sprigs.

Lemongrass Tart

Traditional French *tarte au citron* used to be a great Hammersmith favourite, but we wanted to develop it and so added the lemongrass.

SERVES 8-10
400ml (14fl oz) double cream
2 lemongrass stalks, cut into short lengths and bruised
2 kaffir lime leaves, bruised
400ml (14fl oz) lemon juice (about 10-12 lemons)
4 eggs

400g (14oz) caster sugar
whipped cream, to serve

SWEET SHORTCRUST PASTRY
500g (18oz) plain flour, plus more for dusting
100g (3½oz) caster sugar

200g (7oz) cold butter, diced, plus more for greasing

1 | The night before, put the cream into a small pan and add the lemongrass and lime leaves. Bring to just below the boil, then take off the heat.Cover and leave overnight.

2 | To make the pastry, sift the flour into a large mixing bowl, mix in the sugar and rub the butter in with the fingers or process in a blender until it resembles breadcrumbs, then bring together with a little cold water to form a dough. Leave to rest in the fridge for about 1 hour.

3 | Preheat the oven to 160°C/325°F/gas mark 3 and grease a 25cm (10in) tart pan with butter, then dust it with flour. Roll out the rested pastry and use to line the prepared tart pan. Line that pastry shell with greaseproof paper, weight with beans or rice, and bake blind for 15 minutes.

4 | Meanwhile, in a bowl set over a pan of simmering water (not touching the water), beat the lemon juice, eggs and sugar together until the mixture develops a thick lemon-curdish (rather than custard) consistency. Continue to whisk for a few minutes, then leave to cool a little. Sieve the cream and heat it to roughly the same temperature as the lemon curd, and mix the two together.

5 | Reduce the oven setting to 150°C/300°πF/gas mark 2, pour the mixture into the pastry shell and bake for about 20 minutes, until the filling is set but still has a bit of wobble to it.

6 | Serve with some dollops of whipped cream.

Marsala Figs with Sablé Biscuits

This wonderful combination of flavours and textures makes a truly delightful light summer dessert.

SERVES 4

8 ripe figs, halved
good splash of Marsala
sprinkling of sugar
juice of ¼ lemon
juice of ½ orange

SABLÉ BISCUITS

75g (2¾oz) shelled and skinned hazelnuts
575g (1lb 4½oz) plain flour
300g (10½oz) butter
225g (8oz) icing sugar

a pinch of salt
1 vanilla pod, crushed using a mortar and pestle
3 eggs, lightly beaten

1 | First, gently toss the fig halves in the other ingredients and leave to macerate for at least 1 hour, preferably overnight, turning them carefully from time to time.

2 | To make the sablé biscuits, preheat the oven to 140°C/275°F/gas mark 1 and line a baking tray with baking paper. Grind two-thirds of the nuts finely in a blender or food processor.

3 | Add the rest of the nuts with all the remaining ingredients except the eggs and blend until the mixture has the consistency of fine crumbs.

4 | Add the eggs and knead lightly to a loose paste. Leave to rest for 20 minutes (it will stiffen up in that time).

5 | Spoon the paste into rounds on to the prepared baking tray to make biscuits, spaced well apart to allow for spreading. Cook for 15-20 minutes, until the biscuits are lightly browned around the edges and coming away readily from the baking paper. Leave to cool, then lift from the paper.

6 | Serve two fig halves with each biscuit and drizzle with the Marsala syrup.

Figs

(Ficus carica)

This is another venerable fruit, steeped in history. It has one of the highest sugar contents of all fruits. Fig trees are of the genus *ficus*, of the mulberry family, *moraceae* (and related to both the banyan and breadfruit trees), including the many cultivated varieties of *ficus carica* – the wild fig, originally from western Asia.

Known as the Tree of Knowledge to the ancients, it is no surprise that the fig's leaves supplied the solution to the first awareness of modesty in the Garden of Eden, that Buddha meditated to nirvana under a type of fig tree, and that some Central African tribes adhere to the age-old belief that the spirits of their ancestors live in fig trees.

The *ficus* family does not bear flowers, but instead goes straight to fruit, with all the flowers – more usually thought of as seeds – growing within the velvety edible vase-shaped pods. In the wild, the fig tree is dependent on the tiny fig wasp for pollination. The same is true of the varieties of figs, such as the *smyrna* and *san pedro*, which have been cultivated for thousands of year in western Asia, the Middle East and Mediterranean Europe, and so they need to be grown near wild fig trees, where the wasps are hatched. The pollination process is still favoured in these cases as it is held to give the figs a fuller nuttier flavour.

Most cultivation, though, is of the common fig – which is propagated by cuttings and thus has no need of the helpful wasp. There are literally hundreds of varieties, with many colours, sizes and flavours. Generally there are two crops, a small one bearing larger fruit in the early summer, and another a few months later (sometimes as late as November) bearing much smaller, juicier and sweeter fruit. A large part of this second crop generally goes for drying.

Much prized as a snack and sweetmeat, figs are widely used in cooking, especially in puddings, jams, pickles and other preserves, and in the baking of cakes, breads, pastries and biscuits. We like to bake them and make compotes by poaching them with other fruits in aromatic syrups. They are also delicious macerated in sweet fortified wines, such as Marsala, and chargrilled or barbecued bathed in flavoursome syrups.

Look for plump fruit that are evenly coloured and that give slightly when pressed. As figs are highly perishable, they are usually harvested, transported and sold still slightly under-ripe. They will, however, ripen rapidly if left at room temperature – although nothing can ever taste quite as good as a fig that has been ripened to perfection on the tree.

Figs have a wide range of heath benefits: long held to be a potent internal cleanser, science has more recently shown that this is indeed the case and that figs not only promote the growth of beneficial bacteria in the gut, but also actively destroy bad bacteria and absorb potentially harmful toxins so that they are safely excreted. Figs are also among the richest sources of calcium in the vegetable world.

Ginger Pudding with Toffee Sauce

This version of a traditional steamed sponge pudding has become yet another Gate classic that we dare not take off the menu.

SERVES 6-8

3 eggs, separated
85g (3oz) butter, melted
finely grated zest of 1 lime
150g (5½oz) caster sugar
125g (4½oz) stem ginger, puréed in
  1 tbsp of the syrup

2 tsp ground cinnamon
1 tbsp ground ginger
2 tsp baking powder
275g (9½oz) self-raising flour
300ml (10fl oz) warm milk
double cream, to serve

TOFFEE SAUCE
125g (4½oz) demerara sugar
100g (3½oz) butter
125ml (4fl oz) double cream

1 | Preheat the oven to 190°C/375°F/gas mark 5. In a blender or food processor, cream together the egg yolks, butter and lime zest with the sugar until pale and light. Add the ginger purée and mix in well.

2 | Sift together the spices, baking powder and flour. With the machine running, add the flour mixture and milk in alternating spoonfuls, until all of both is incorporated.

3 | Beat the egg whites until standing in stiff peaks, then fold them gently into the flour mixture.

4 | Line a large pudding basin or six to eight individual pudding moulds with greaseproof paper and spoon the mixture into it or them, until about two-thirds full. Cover with greaseproof paper cut to fit the top(s).

5 | Put in a deep baking tray half-filled with hot water and cook in the oven for 45 minutes for the individual puddings and 60 minutes for a large one (a skewer inserted into the heart of the pudding will come out dry).

6 | While the pudding(s) cook(s), make the sauce. Put all the ingredients in a heavy-based pan and heat gently, stirring from to time, until the butter has melted and the sugar dissolved, then bring just to the boil and leave to cool.

7 | Take the paper tops off the cooked puddings, then turn them out on to serving plates and remove the lining paper. Spoon the toffee sauce over and around the pudding(s), then drizzle some cream around to decorate.

Passion Fruit and Hazlenut Roulade

This technique is based on the way Adrian's old pâtissière friend, George, made flourless sponges for chocolate cakes. We use various versions of it to make desserts for our wheat-sensitive regulars.

SERVES 4-6

melted butter, for brushing
5 eggs, separated
85g (3oz) caster sugar, plus 2 tbsp
    finely grated zest of 1 orange
100g (3½oz) shelled and skinned
    hazelnuts, coarsely chopped

FILLING
250ml (9fl oz) double cream
pulp from 12 passion fruit
1 tbsp icing sugar or to taste, plus
    more to decorate (optional)
splash of Grand Marnier (optional)

1 | Preheat the oven to 180°C/350°F/gas mark 4. Line a medium-sized lipped baking sheet with baking parchment, then brush it with melted butter.

2 | Beat the egg whites with half the sugar until you have soft peaks.

3 | In a bowl set over simmering water, beat the egg yolks with the rest of the sugar until they become slightly thickened and paler in colour. Gently fold into the egg whites with a spatula until well mixed. Mix in the orange zest and one-third of the nuts.

4 | Spoon into the prepared baking sheet – it should be about 1cm (½in) deep – and cook in the oven for about 15 minutes, until nicely browned and beginning to come away from the edges.

5 | Lay a sheet of baking parchment slightly bigger than the baking tray out on a work surface and sprinkle it with the nuts, then the 2 tbsp sugar.

6 | Invert the meringue on top of the nut-and-sugar-dusted paper and quickly and carefully loosen the lining paper, but leave it in place until ready to spread. Allow to cool – the meringue will sink, but don't worry.

7 | For the filling, beat the cream to soft peaks and sweeten the passion fruit with the icing sugar if necessary (it shouldn't be too sweet – you need some of its tartness to balance the sweet meringue). Mix about two-thirds of the passion fruit pulp into the cream, along with the liqueur if you are using it, and spread over the base in a thin layer.

8 | Starting from one long side, use the paper to roll up the meringue into a cylinder. Roll it up tightly in the paper, twist the ends to seal and chill in the fridge for about an hour.

9 | Cut across into eight to twelve slices, arrange two slices on top of each other on each serving plate and spoon over the remaining passion fruit pulp. Dust with icing sugar if you like.

Chocolate Fondant with Prunes in Armagnac

This is one of those dishes in which several flavours that are wonderful in their own right blend together to produce something remarkable. Digging your spoon into this pud reveals a gooey chocolatey mass that is as alluring as it is tasty. You can make one big pudding instead of the small ones, but it will take longer to cook – about 15 minutes. Don't serve more than a fifth of this big pud to anyone or use the mix to make less than five small puddings, as it is so rich and dense they will not be able to finish it!

SERVES 5-6

about 18 good-quality stoned prunes
50ml (2fl oz) Armagnac
350g (12oz) good-quality dark chocolate (minimum 70% cocoa solids), finely chopped
100g (3½oz) unsalted butter, diced
150g (5½oz) caster sugar
4 eggs
55g (2oz) plain flour, sifted
pinch of salt

1 | Well ahead, ideally the night before, soak the prunes in the Armagnac.

2 | Preheat the oven to 230°C/450°F/gas mark 8 and line five to six small pudding bowls or large ramekins with foil.

3 | Melt the chocolate in a large bowl set over a pan of gently simmering water, but not in contact with the water.

4 | In another large bowl, beat the butter and sugar together until the colour of the mixture goes pale. Stir in the eggs one at a time, making sure that each is well amalgamated before adding the next. Finally sift in the flour with the salt and mix in well.

5 | Mix one-third of the flour mixture into the chocolate and blend well. Add this back to the bowl of flour mixture and fold in lightly with a metal spoon until uniform in colour. Stir in the prunes and any remaining unabsorbed liquid.

6 | Spoon the mixture into the prepared bowls or ramekins – they shouldn't be much more than half full. Cook in the hot oven for about 12 minutes, until the top looks baked and is cracking in several places. Don't cook for any longer, as if you do the filling will not be nice and gooey.

Chocolate Pecan Truffle Cake

This icon for chocolate addicts is unfortunately not suitable for children, pregnant women, the elderly or invalids, as it contains raw eggs.

SERVES 6

200g (7oz) shelled pecan nuts
75g (2¾oz) unsalted butter, plus
  extra for greasing
400g (14oz) good-quality dark
  chocolate (minimum 70% cocoa
  solids), finely chopped
300ml (10fl oz) double cream
7 egg whites

1 | Well ahead, ideally the night before, toast the pecans gently in a dry frying pan until browned and aromatic. Tip on to a flat plate and leave to cool. Chop coarsely.

2 | Line an 18cm (7in) springform cake pan with baking paper and grease that with butter.

3 | Melt the butter and chocolate in a large bowl set over a pan of gently simmering water, but not in contact with the water. Allow to cool, then beat in the cream.

4 | Beat the egg whites until standing in stiff peaks. Fold about 3 tbsp of the beaten egg whites into the chocolate mixture to loosen it, then gently fold in the rest with the edge of a metal spoon. Gently fold in the nuts in the same way.

5 | Pour into the prepared cake pan and chill for at least 6 hours, or preferably overnight.

Chocolate Bread and Butter Pudding

This is a real comfort pud, as it has all the classic nice things in it. Use any chocolate *crème anglaise* left over to decorate the pudding.

SERVES 4

300g (10½oz) brioche, cut across into 1cm (½in) slices
1½ recipe quantities *crème anglaise* (page 228), made using 8 egg yolks
100g (3½oz) good-quality dark chocolate (minimum 70% cocoa solids), broken into pieces
5 tbsp whole milk

55g (2oz) caster sugar
55g (2oz) butter
3 bananas, peeled and sliced
55g (2oz) shelled macadamia nuts, roasted and coarsely chopped
fruit *coulis* (page 228) of choice, to serve
chocolate shavings, to decorate

CARAMELIZED BANANAS (OPTIONAL)
1 banana
demerara sugar

1 | For the best results, soak the brioche slices in the two-thirds of the *crème anglaise*, covered in the refrigerator, overnight.

2 | Preheat the oven to 180°C/350°F/gas mark 4. In a pan, heat the chocolate in the milk with the sugar and butter, whisking fairly constantly. Mix this mixture into the remaining *crème anglaise*.

3 | Dip the banana slices into the chocolate *crème anglaise*.

4 | In each of four dariole moulds lined with greaseproof paper, layer up the brioche soaked in *crème anglaise* followed by slices of banana dipped in the chocolate *crème anglaise* to cover, together with a good splash of the chocolate *crème anglaise*, followed by a sprinkling of nuts. Continue with the layers until you reach the top of the mould, pressing down each firmly. Pour in the remaining (non-chocolate-flavoured) *crème anglaise* into each mould until it just comes to the top.

5 | Bake in a bain-marie (or simply a deep baking tray half-filled with boiling water) in the oven for about 30 minutes, until just lightly set (the tip of a knife comes out clean).

6 | Serve warm set on a pool of fruit *coulis*, with chocolate shavings to decorate. If you want to add the caramelized bananas, slice the banana at an angle into long oval slices, sprinkle these with demerara sugar and blowtorch or griddle on both sides until the sugar caramelizes.

Baklava with Cardamom and Rose Water

Ideally make this baklava two to three days before you need it, as the flavour and texture really improve in that time.

MAKES 50-60 PIECES
600g (1lb 5oz) shelled pistachios, chopped, plus more to serve
600g (1lb 5oz) shelled almonds, skinned and chopped
200ml (7fl oz) vegetable oil

SHORTCRUST PASTRY
1kg (2¼lb) plain flour
pinch of salt
400g (14oz) cold butter, diced
100ml (3½fl oz) iced water

SYRUP
500g (18oz) caster sugar
seeds from 5 green cardamom pods
5 tbsp rose water

1 | First make the pastry. Sift the flour into a large mixing bowl and stir in the salt. Rub in the butter with the fingertips until the mixture resembles coarse crumbs. Add all but 1-2 spoonfuls of the water and cut it into the mix with a knife. Gather together with your hands and, if it feels too crumbly, add just a little more water and repeat the cutting-in process until it begins to form a coherent mass. Bring together as a ball and chill for at least 30 minutes to make it easier to work with.

2 | Preheat the oven to 180°C/350°F/gas mark 4. Cut the dough into four and roll out each piece, one at a time. Roll the first slightly thicker and use to line the bottom of a deep 40cm (16in) round cake pan. Trim off any excess. Scatter half the pistachios evenly over this pastry. Roll the second piece of dough slightly thinner, place over the pistachio layer and press down firmly all round. Trim off any thick edge or excess that goes up the sides. Scatter the almonds over that and repeat with another thinner layer of pastry. Scatter the remaining pistachios over that and finish with a slightly thicker round of pastry. Press down each layer firmly and trim off any thicker edges or pastry that goes up the sides.

3 | With a long sharp knife, slice across the pastry all the way down to the bottom at 2.5cm (1in) intervals. Rotate the pan by 60 degrees and repeat to make lozenge shapes (some of the pastry layers may come up with the knife as you do this, simply arrange them back in place).

4 | Pour the vegetable oil evenly over the pastry and bake for 1½ hours, until evenly coloured a light golden brown.

5 | Meanwhile, make the syrup. In a heavy-based pan, dissolve the sugar in 500ml (18fl oz) water. Add the cardamom seeds, bring to the boil and boil rapidly for 2-3 minutes. Leave to cool and, when cool, strain and stir in the rose water.

6 | Take the pastry out of the oven, pour the syrup evenly over it and leave to cool completely. Leave at least until the next day, better still three to four days, before serving.

7 | Sprinkle with more chopped pistachios to serve as petits fours after a meal, as a dessert, or with tea or coffee.

Elderflower Pavlova

If you can't get a hold of fresh elderflowers to make this lovely pud, you can use a few tablespoons of elderflower cordial. If you do, cut down the amount of sugar you use, as the beauty of this dessert is the way the elderflower flavour cuts the sweetness of the meringue.

SERVES 6

4 egg whites
240g (8½oz) caster sugar
1 tsp white wine vinegar
3 tbsp fresh elderflowers,
 stems snipped off

150ml (5fl oz) double cream
150g (5½oz) mascarpone cheese
300g (10½oz) mixed summer berries
mint sprigs, to decorate

1 | Preheat the oven to 150°C/300°F/gas mark 2, and line a baking sheet with greaseproof paper. Beat the egg whites with the sugar and vinegar until standing in stiff peaks, then gently fold in the elderflowers.

2 | Pipe this meringue into four 8cm (3¼in) discs on the prepared baking sheet and put in the oven for about 2 hours until the meringues come away from the paper with ease. Leave to cool.

3 | Mix the cream and mascarpone, spoon into the meringue discs and top with the berries. Garnish with mint sprigs.

Halva with Paratha

This sweet treat is traditional at Jewish New Year in India and Iraq.

SERVES 6-8
300g (10½oz) caster sugar
seeds from 4 cardamom pods,
  crushed
pinch of saffron strands
3 tbsp rose water
425g (15oz) semolina

100g (3½oz) butter
75g (2¾oz) flaked almonds, toasted
55g (2oz) shelled pistachios, toasted
55g (2oz) sultanas, soaked in hot
  water for 10 minutes

PARATHA
125g (4½oz) each of chapati flour and
  plain flour
1 tsp salt
a little vegetable oil
125g (4½oz) butter, softened

1 | Start by making the *paratha* dough. In a bowl, mix the flours and salt with just enough warm water to give a workable dough. Knead for 3-4 minutes, then gather into a ball, oil lightly and leave to rest in a warm place in the bowl, covered with a clean cloth, for 30-40 minutes.

2 | Preheat the oven to 190°C/375°F/gas mark 5. Put the sugar, cardamom seeds, saffron and rose water in a saucepan with 500ml (18fl oz) water over a gentle heat and stir until the sugar dissolves, then bring to a simmer and cook gently for about 10 minutes.

3 | Meanwhile, toast the semolina in a heavy-based pan over a gentle heat, stirring and tossing from time to time, until all of it is lightly browned – about 10-12 minutes.

4 | In a small pan, melt the butter and cook gently for 2-3 minutes, then increase the heat and cook until it just begins to turn brown.

5 | Scatter all the nuts over a baking sheet and brown for about 6 minutes in the preheated oven.

6 | Meanwhile, mix the butter into the semolina and carry on cooking over a low heat, stirring frequently, until everything is well mixed. Then add the cardamom syrup and mix in well. Leave to cook over a low heat, stirring from time to time, for about 10-15 minutes, until the semolina is cooked – test a few grains to see if they are soft.

7 | Mix in the nuts and sultanas and spoon into a large shallow bowl, smooth the surface and leave to cool.

8 | To finish the *parathas*, cut the rested dough into largish billiard-ball shapes and roll each to a round about 2mm (⅟₁₆in) thick. Brush the top of each paratha with soft butter, fold into half and butter the top again, then into quarters and butter yet again. Roll out to a flat disc again and then repeat the whole process of buttering, folding and rolling three times (it's a bit like making puff pastry). Finally, roll out into rounds about 3-4cm (1¼-1½in) thick and cook in a very hot frying pan for 2-3 minutes on each side, until nicely browned and puffed slightly. Set aside in warm place.

9 | Serve the halva with a paratha on the side to be eaten almost like hummus and pitta bread.

Chargrilled Fruit with Lemongrass Syrup

This updated take on the fruit salad makes a perfect way to finish a barbecue meal.

SERVES 4

½ pineapple, peeled, cored and cut into thick slices
1 banana, peeled and cut at an angle into long slices
2 large strawberries, hulled and halved

2 nectarines, halved and stones removed
2 figs, halved
1 sharon fruit, quartered
mint, to garnish
vanilla ice-cream, to serve

LEMONGRASS SYRUP
3 lemongrass stalks, finely chopped and pounded in a pestle and mortar
200g (7oz) caster sugar
juice of 1 lime

1 | To make the lemongrass syrup, put the lemongrass and sugar in a pan, add 250ml (9fl oz) water, stir to dissolve the sugar then bring to the boil and simmer for at least 20 minutes. Take off the heat once it has a good sticky consistency, and stir in the lime juice.

2 | Grill, griddle or barbecue the fruits until nicely seared. As they begin to soften, drizzle them with some of the syrup to caramelize the surfaces.

3 | Serve drizzled with a little more syrup, decorated with some fresh mint and accompanied by vanilla ice-cream.

Pineapple and Chilli Crumble

Crumbles continue to be among the most popular of our desserts. We always serve this one as individual servings, moulded in mousse rings, as you can then see the layers nicely. It is, however, just as good and tasty as one big crumble in a large dish. You can re-use the sugar syrup afterwards for poaching more fruit or for sweetening a fruit coulis.

SERVES 4
2-3 crisp pears, peeled, cored and cut into chunks
½ ripe pineapple, peeled, cored, sliced and cut into chunks
crème anglaise **(page 228) or double cream, to serve**

CHILLI SUGAR SYRUP
1 star anise
75g (2¾oz) caster sugar
1 medium red chilli, seeded and finely chopped

CRUMBLE TOPPING
100g (3½oz) cold butter, cubed
100g (3½oz) plain flour
100g (3½oz) ground almonds
75g (2¾oz) caster sugar
pinch of ground cinnamon

1 | Preheat the oven to 190°C/375°F/gas mark 5. To make the chilli sugar syrup, put the star anise and sugar in a small pan with 300ml (10fl oz) water. Bring to the boil, stirring to dissolve the sugar, and simmer for another couple of minutes.

2 | Add the pears and poach gently for anything from 5-25 minutes, depending on the variety of pear and how ripe they are, until just tender. Remove from the syrup using a slotted spoon.

3 | Add the chilli to the syrup and simmer for about 3 minutes, until the chilli has softened and the stock has reduced slightly and developed a reddish hue.

4 | Add the pineapple to the chillied syrup and simmer for 2 minutes, just to caramelize it slightly and infuse it with the chilli flavour.

5 | Meanwhile, make the crumble topping by rubbing the butter into the other ingredients or whizzing everything in a food processor, until the mixture resembles breadcrumbs.

6 | Mix the pears and pineapple and pile into either a soufflé dish or four small bowls, mousse moulds or pastry rings, packing it down well if using the moulds or rings. Spoon the topping over the fruit and cook in the preheated oven for 10-12 minutes until the topping is nicely browned.

7 | To serve, push the individual crumbles out of the moulds or rings, if using them, and serve with some *crème anglaise* or double cream.

Drinks

Among the most popular items on our drinks menu are the non-alcoholic drinks we make from fruit, vegetables, herbs and spices. Their aromatic fresh flavours can waft you away to another world.

Ginger Spritzer

This is the ultimate expression of the refreshing qualities of ginger.

MAKES 10 GLASSES
100g (3½oz) caster sugar
large wedge of fresh root ginger
ice, to serve
sparkling mineral water, to serve
fresh lime juice, to serve (optional)

1 | For the sugar syrup, put the sugar in a small pan with 100ml (3½fl oz) water. Bring to the boil, stirring, and simmer for another couple of minutes.

2 | Peel the ginger, chop it coarsely into chunks and add to the sugar syrup. Bring back to the boil, take off the heat and leave to macerate overnight.

3 | Put 2-3 tbsp of the strained ginger syrup into the bottom of a tall glass with some ice and top up with sparkling mineral water. Add a bit of lime juice to taste if you like.

Mint Tea

This is an increasingly popular drink, particularly served as a *digestif* after a meal.

MAKES 1 GLASS
small handful of fresh mint leaves
boiling water
1 good-quality tea bag, such as
  English breakfast (optional)
4-5 tsp sugar, to taste

1 | Put the mint leaves in a tall heatproof glass, pour in boiling water and leave to infuse for about 5 minutes. For more colour and added whoomph, dip the tea bag in just after adding the boiling water (you can use the same tea bag for several glasses).

2 | Stir in the sugar, or more or less to taste, and serve.

Fruit and Vegetable Juices

We make a range of these using single flavours such as carrot and apple – or a mixture of the two (sometimes with a little fresh root ginger), such as beetroot and celery. Indeed a mixture of beetroot, carrot and celery is one of our best sellers. There is not much to say about making these, except that you do need a proper heavy-duty juicer and for an average large glass of juice you'll need 400-500g (14-18oz) of fruit and/or veg.

Sharbat-idana

This is a special drink our Grandmother would make for special family parties and gatherings. For us kids, the really exciting thing was the addition of the tiny black tukmaria seeds which, when soaked in water, wouldswell up to make what we thought seemed like little furry tadpoles and neverfailed to fascinate us. Tukmaria or sabja seeds, also known moreromantically in some quarters as 'tiger tiger', can be found in good Asianand Middle Eastern stores; if you can't find them, the drink is just as tasty without, but will lack the same kid appeal. Gran used to add some red food colouring to boost the colour of the drink, but what we do is add a few slices of fresh beetroot to the cooling syrup.

MAKES ABOUT 10 GLASSES
1 tbsp tukmaria seeds (see above)
sugar syrup as above
few slices of fresh beetroot
 (optional)
3 tbsp rose water
a little rose essence
ice, to serve
still mineral water, to serve
lime juice, to serve (optional)

1 | Put the tukmaria seeds in a small bowl and add about 300ml (10fl oz) cold water. Leave to soak overnight. Make the syrup, adding the beetroot slices as it cools for colour if you like.

2 | Put 2-3 tbsp of the sieved syrup into tall glasses together with 1 tsp of the rose water, a few drops of rose essence, 2-3 tsp of the tukmaria mixture and some ice. Top up with still mineral water to serve. If you like, stir a few drops of lime juice into each glass to taste.

Index

Detailed treatments of certain foods and methods are shown in **bold** typeface.